Evaluating
Social Science Research

An Introduction

Thomas R. Black

SAGE Publications

London · Thousand Oaks · New Delhi

First published 1993

SAGE Publications Ltd
6 Bonhill Street
London EC2A 4PU

SAGE Publications Inc
2455 Teller Road
Thousand Oaks, California 91320

SAGE Publications India Pvt Ltd
32, M-Block Market
Greater Kailash – I
New Delhi 110 048

British Library Cataloguing in Publication data

Black, Thomas, R.
  Evaluating Social Science Research:
  Introduction
  I. Title
  300.7

  ISBN 0–8039–8852–4
  ISBN 0–8039–8853–2 (pbk)

Library of Congress catalog card number 93–085034

Typeset by Photoprint, Torquay, Devon
Printed in Great Britain by Redwood Books, Trowbridge,
Wiltshire

Contents

Preface

The aim of this book is to provide the knowledge and skills necessary to read and evaluate research reports, journal articles and conference papers which include some aspect of measurement. It has been written for anyone in education or the social sciences, but with postgraduate students in education and final year/postgraduate students in psychology or sociology particularly in mind. It is not the primary goal of this book to teach how to design research, though much of what is included here should prepare new researchers to be aware of many of the pitfalls in designing, carrying out and reporting research, as well as providing a sound background in basic concepts related to research design. Thus the book should provide the prerequisites for anyone wishing to pursue a more traditional first course in statistics for social science research.

While the book can be read on its own, it was designed to be used as the basis of a course for those whose main concern is reading the literature intelligently and critically. The advantage of using it as part of a course comes from the interaction with others. The aims of the book are at a high cognitive level: to acquire evaluation skills. It can also be used as a complementary book for a more traditional course in statistics and research design. There are definite benefits in discussing one's analysis with others, with or without the guidance of an 'expert', but there will be little chance of achieving the objectives of this set of materials if it is taken as just another book to be read. These skills require practice to master, which means actually dissecting articles and papers.

A course on evaluating research can be an end in itself (there are more consumers of research than producers), or a precursor to a course on research design methodology or statistics. All students and researchers should read broadly, including literature that describes tools and approaches that they have no intention of using themselves. Therefore, even if there is no intent to carry out a measurement- and statistically based study, everyone should be able to read about other research that has used statistics, with not only basic understanding, but with a critical eye. This book aims to prepare you to do just that.

For those interested in greater depth, this book can be used in conjunction with such texts as Kerlinger (1986) or Cohen and Manion (1989), formal studies on research design. A more mathematical approach (though still quite elementary) could be achieved by using Rowntree (1981), or with such texts as Chase (1985) or Blalock (1979) forming the basis of a traditional introductory statistics course. The choice of depth is up to the individual, and numerous references are made to other texts to assist the reader in pursuing topics further.

Part of my motivation for writing this text has come from encounters over the years with postgraduate research students and colleagues who have fought shy of reading articles with statistics in them. Some have actually expressed a fear of statistics, having apparently had bad experiences with numbers in their youth. Others have voiced sincere doubts about the use of statistics, some of which I share when reading certain articles and papers. No tool is universally applicable to all problems, and there have been some notable occasions when quantitative data have been collected in situations that were not appropriate and 'statistically' analysed. But as a scientist I would prefer any doubt to be rationally based, allowing one to have an open mind when reading a report of a research project.

The book is organized so that the first chapter provides an overview of the research process and an outline of the skills and knowledge to be covered. Subsequent chapters introduce the concepts and criteria for evaluating the various aspects of research. Each chapter contains two types of Activities: the first is intended to help clarify new concepts and criteria, while the second (at the end of each chapter) actually involves readers in the critical analysis and evaluation of research reports. This second type of Activity should be carried out on one or more articles or parts of reports the reader may find in the literature. These will require the reader to use progressively more columns (sets of criteria) on the Profiling Sheet, a complete copy of which is found at the end of Chapter 8. Some of these could be used for formal assessment in a course of study. The idea of using a Profiling Sheet to guide researchers in the critical analysis and evaluation of research reports is not original, the author used a simpler one as a postgraduate student (Gephart and Bartos, 1969) and found it immensely useful.

If this book is used with classes or seminars, optimally three sessions (about an hour each) per chapter are needed, one to discuss the concepts and another two for comparison analyses of articles. To what depth the analysis is carried will determine the amount of out-of-class reading necessary in addition to the chapters of this book. There is the potential for about 100–130 hours of activity to be generated by reading this book and carrying out all the Activities, depending on background and previous experience.

I wish to thank the groups of postgraduate students who used earlier versions of this text, offering most useful comments and criticism. In particular, thanks go to colleagues Joan Dean and David Gray who went though drafts, providing detailed analysis and valuable ideas for improvements. As is always the case, ultimate responsibility for the content and style still lies with the author.

Thomas R. Black
University of Surrey

References

Blalock, H.M. (1979) *Social Statistics*, rev. 2nd edn. McGraw-Hill Kogakusha.

Chase, C.I. (1985) *Elementary Statistical Procedures*, 3rd edn. McGraw-Hill.

Cohen, L. and Manion, L. (1989) *Research Methods in Education*, 3rd edn. Routledge.

Gephart, W.J. and Bartos, B.B. (1969) *Occasional Paper 7: Profiling Instructional Package.* Phi Delta Kappa.

Kerlinger, F.N. (1986) *Foundations of Behavioral Research*, 3rd edn. Holt, Rinehart & Winston.

Rowntree, D. (1981) *Statistics without Tears: a Primer for Non-mathematicians*. Penguin.

1
Evaluating Social Science Research: an Overview

Social science research involves investigating all aspects of human activity and interactivity. Considering academic disciplines, psychology tends to investigate the behaviour of individuals, while sociology examines groups and their characteristics. Educational research can be viewed as an endeavour to expand understanding of teaching/learning situations, covering the cognitive, affective and psychomotor domains, thus drawing upon the perceptions of both psychology and sociology. Ideally, the research community should be able to address itself to general, global questions, such as what enhances learning in primary school, what contributes to poverty, why do individuals engage in crime, which would in turn generate a set of specific research questions. To resolve such issues would require researchers to choose the appropriate research tool or tools for the chosen specific question(s). Individual researchers (or teams) would select an aspect of the problem of interest that it was feasible to tackle with the resources available. Their contribution would then be added to the growing body of knowledge accumulating through the combined efforts of the research community. To a certain extent, this does happen, but unfortunately the social sciences seem less able to achieve such a coherent approach to research than some other academic fields.

This shortcoming stems at least partly from the fact that carrying out social science research involves considering many more variables, some of which are often difficult, if not impossible, to control. This is unlike research in the natural sciences which commonly takes place in a laboratory under conditions where control over potentially contributing factors is more easily exercised. Secondly, there is less widespread agreement about underlying theories and appropriate methods for resolving issues in the social sciences than in many disciplines. Consequently, a wide variety of measuring instruments, research tools and approaches can be employed, some of which seem unnecessarily complicated. The complexities and idiosyncrasies of social science research present a challenge for the person new to the field.

Adding to the difficulty of extracting the most out of published research are the various 'schools of thought' relating to social science research. On a public level, note the dissonance between clinical and experimental psychologists. In some academic departments, staff who 'use statistics' have not been spoken to by their colleagues – who 'never touch the stuff' –

for years. On an intellectual level, there has been considerable discussion about such schisms. Cohen and Manion (1989) present a comprehensive introduction leading to the classification of two research 'paradigms', though not all researchers conveniently admit to belonging to one or other, or even to fitting the categories. Historically, these derive from objectivist (realism, positivism, determinism, nomothetic) and subjectivist (nominalism, anti-positivism, voluntarism, ideographic) schools of thought. Briefly, as Cohen and Manion (1989: 38) note:

> The normative paradigm (or model) contains two major orienting ideas: first, that human behaviour is essentially *rule-governed*; and second, that it should be investigated by the *methods of natural science*. The interpretive paradigm, in contrast to its normative counterpart, is characterised by a *concern for the individual*. Whereas normative studies are positivist, all theories constructed within the context of the interpretive paradigm tend to be anti-positivist.

Though the anti-positivists level the criticism that science tends to be dehumanizing, it can be argued that science (or more appropriately, a scientific approach) is a means not an end; with it we can both better understand the human condition and predict the consequences of action, generalized to some degree. How this understanding is used or what action is taken will be based upon values, the realm of philosophy. Thus it may not be science that depersonalizes, but the values that the people who apply it have; if there is any corruption of the human spirit, it lies in beliefs and human nature, not in a scientific approach. To recall an old ditty based upon a murder case in New England in 1892,

> Lizzie Borden took an axe
> And gave her mother forty whacks
> And when she saw what she had done
> She gave her father forty-one.

To say that science is evil is like convicting the axe, instead of the murderer who used it as a tool for the destruction of human life.

Science is no more susceptible to abuse in the form of depersonalization and human degradation than any other competing intellectual endeavour. We have seen, and still see, wars in the name of God, carried out by virtually every major religion in the world, most of which have a major tenet against killing. There has been and will be oppression in the name of political systems that purport to represent and protect the masses, resulting in everything from dictatorships of the proletariat under Communism to restrictive voting practices to 'protect' so-called democratic societies. Science or a scientific approach in viewing the world, like religion, political theory or humanistic psychology, is a means to understanding, and is depersonalizing in the study of people only if the social scientist wants it to be.

One goal of scientific research is to be self-policing through rigour and consistency of practice. This is necessary if the conclusions drawn at the end of a piece of complex research are to be valid and replicable. Logical consistency from one stage to another, combined with reliable procedures, is essential. While achievement of this goal through so-called good practice is implicit in any study, scientific research is just as prone to bias and/or poor practice as any approach. The unresolved case of Cyril Burt's studies of identical twins comes to mind, unresolved in the sense that there is no conclusive evidence that he falsified his data, but there is strong statistical evidence that he did. As Blum and Foos (1986) note, scientists are human beings and susceptible to common foibles including stupidity and dishonesty. They summarize their view of the academic world as follows:

> Whereas some scientists espouse the view of a self-correcting mechanism whereby scientific inquiry is subject to rigorous policing, others believe that academic research centers foster intense pressure to publish, to obtain research and renewal of grants, or to qualify for promotion. Still others believe that finagling is endemic and that public exposure is to be continually encouraged.

This does not mean that there is widespread fraud and that reading research reports is like trying to buy a used car from a politician. Evaluating research requires a more measured approach: many reports will have faults, most will provide some valuable insights, but judging the validity of these will require knowing what to look for.

There are limitations to both 'paradigms', particularly when applied in isolation from one another. Poorly conducted, normative studies can produce findings that are so trivial as to contribute little to the body of research. On the other hand, interpretive studies can be so isolated, subjective and idiosyncratic that there is no hope of any generalization or contribution to a greater body of knowledge. When ideologies are taken to lesser extremes, it can be said that the two paradigms complement each other, rather than compete. To choose one as the basis of research prior to planning may be a philosophical decision, but it could also be likened to opening the tool box, choosing a spanner and ignoring the other tools available when faced with a repair task. To reject the findings of researchers who appear to subscribe to a supposed opposing paradigm is to ignore a considerable body of work. Cohen and Manion (1989: 42–3) summarize the position nicely when closing their discussion of the subject:

> we will restrict its [the term research] usages to those activities and undertakings aimed at developing *a science of behaviour*, the word 'science' itself implying both normative and interpretive perspectives. Accordingly, when we speak of social research, we have in mind the systematic and scholarly application of the principles of a science of behaviour to the problems of man within his social context; and when we use the term educational research, we likewise have in mind the application of these self same principles to the problems of teaching and learning within the formal educational framework and to the clarification of issues having direct or indirect bearing on these concepts.

The particular value of scientific research, as defined above, in the social sciences, is that it will enable researchers and consumers of the research to develop the kind of sound knowledge base that characterizes other professions and disciplines. It should be one that will ensure that all the disciplines which are concerned with enhancing understanding of human interaction and behaviour will acquire a maturity and sense of progression which they seem to lack at present.

This book will address the issue of evaluating the quality of a major subset of social science research: that involving various forms of observation and measurement (some of which will employ statistics as a decision-making aid). This covers some aspect of most social science research since the majority involves collecting data of one form or another, and all data gathering should be well defined and verifiable (Blum and Foos, 1986). While this begs the issue as to which 'paradigm' is being employed, it does mean that the criteria and evaluation approaches described here will apply to some aspects of all studies that collect data, quantifiable or not. Consequently, this book leaves out philosophical studies, assuming that they do not refer to observation- or measurement-based research.

There are two practical reasons for emphasizing this aspect of social science research. The first is to assist readers in overcoming the problem of interpreting existing publications containing data, numerical and qualitative. The second is to assist designers of research, since the cause of much low-quality social science research (and not just statistically based studies) is often rooted in problems of measurement and data collection. Too often, new researchers base their techniques unquestioningly upon the practices of others. They read the research reports and journal articles and assume that if they are published, they must have followed acceptable procedures. This is not a sound assumption in an age when academics suffer from the 'publish or perish' syndrome, and not all journal referees are equally proficient in separating the wheat from the chaff.

It is not a trivial task to analyse a research paper critically. There can be errors of omission as well as faulty logic and poor procedure. Many of these must be inferred from reading a written discourse and their relative severity weighed against some vague standard of acceptability. Like most complex skills, proficiency at evaluating studies will be acquired through practice and application to a variety of situations. Hence the considerable number of Activities built into the present material. As with most higher level skills, the acquisition of these can benefit from discussions and interaction with fellow researchers. Therefore, as most of the Activities focus on the discussion and evaluation of research papers, it is desirable to have a forum in which to defend and justify your position, in order to ensure that your logic and criteria are sound. This can be done in a class or tutorial, or simply by discussing an article with a friend.

In general, the consumer of research reports should learn to be critical without being hypercritical and pedantic, able to ascertain the important aspects, ignore the trivia and, to a certain extent, read between the lines by making appropriate inferences. The ability to identify true omissions and overt commissions of errors is a valuable skill. It is not so much a matter of right and wrong, but one of considering relative quality. No research is going to be perfectly carried out and reported but, at the other extreme,

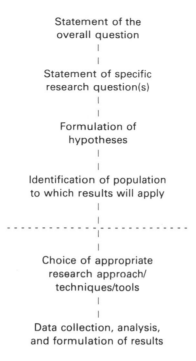

Statement of the
overall question

Statement of specific
research question(s)

Formulation of
hypotheses

Identification of population
to which results will apply

Choice of appropriate
research approach/
techniques/tools

Data collection, analysis,
and formulation of results

Figure 1.1   *Summary of the processes of designing and carrying out educational/social science research.*

little published material will be totally useless. Therefore, as consumers, we must be able to ascertain the worthwhile and ignore the erroneous without rejecting everything.

Research designs

Regardless of which research model is eventually chosen, all research endeavours have some traits in common. This is based on the assumption that the primary purpose is to expand knowledge and understanding. It is doubtful that an endeavour to justify a stand regardless of the evidence available can be considered research: these are the domains of irrational opinion, beliefs and politics. Figure 1.1 outlines the key components of any research activity, though the actual order of events may vary somewhat from the sequence shown and each step may be visited more than once, the researcher reconsidering a decision having changed his/her mind, or wishing to refine a point. Beginning at the top, an *overall question* will have arisen in the potential researcher's mind, based on previous experience(s), reading and/or observations. For example, what enhances learning, why do people forget, what social conditions contribute to crime, what influence on attitudes does television have?

For a researcher to begin a project with no question formulated but with a research approach already chosen, like a case study, survey or statistical model, is roughly equivalent to opening one's tool box, grasping the favourite hammer, and dashing about to see what needs fixing. On the other hand, this does *not* mean that the statement of the question should be so restrictive as to hamper the quality of the research by placing an unchangeable constraint, but a question does need to be identified to provide a touchstone for subsequent steps in the process. In any case, one would expect when reading a research paper to find a statement of the overall question being addressed, the question to which the researcher intends his results to contribute an answer.

Starting with a general interest area or problem, a *specific research question* should be explicitly stated. This helps to focus attention on the purpose of the research and assists when making decisions about such matters as appropriate research tools. Obviously, the statement of the question could be refined in the light of experience at a later date, if necessary. An informed change of direction in a project is not unheard of, though extreme changes may indicate inadequate initial planning. But putting pencil to paper at an early stage helps to avoid problems arising from ambiguities at a later time. The research question described in a final report, therefore, may have been revised several times. This is quite reasonable; what can be frustrating to a reader is not to find any statement of a research question.

The next stage involves a refined statement of what is expected as the outcome of the research, the *hypotheses*. It is difficult to believe that a researcher would engage in a study when he or she does not have some expectation of the outcome. What is essential is that this is an expectation and not a foregone conclusion. All research approaches have procedures to follow when being carried out and stating hypotheses is one that is common to most. Very little, if any, respected research is totally unstructured and unplanned. Research does not just happen, as Nisbet and Watt (1978: 49) in their description of case studies, underline: 'Both survey and case study involve formulation of hypotheses. Without hypotheses, both become merely a formless and uninformative rag-bag of observations.' Hypotheses help fix the direction of a study and are a more formal way of expressing the research questions. They too can be revised, though which set of tools one eventually chooses may limit how much flexibility there is in changing the specification of hypotheses. The criteria that will define an adequate hypothesis will be discussed in detail later.

Another issue that the reader expects to be addressed early in a study, and described in the report, is *to whom will the results apply*? To what group will the conclusions be relevant? The answer to this may have a strong influence on what research tools are eventually chosen, particularly when the question of the limitations of resources (money, time and effort available) are brought to bear. There are several views about the generalizability of results, deciding to whom do they apply, as will be seen later. The group or *population* (no matter how large or how small) to whom the results will extend needs to be clarified and an adequate justification provided. Issues related to this will be discussed in detail in Chapter 3 as one of the major criteria.

Having looked briefly at characteristics common to all research, the rest of this book will focus on the problems associated with measurement-based studies and those using statistics. Such research will include case studies and surveys where no statistical tests are used, but data are collected in numerical form from observations, questionnaires or other instruments. The only research to which this paper is not relevant is that which generates no data. A word of warning, though: one should not be misled into thinking that just because numbers and statistics are used that a study is trying (or even should be trying) to establish causality. Statistical techniques are a tool that might be used as *part* of an argument for establishing causality, or for establishing an explanation.

A brief word on statistics

Regardless of which approach is eventually chosen for resolving a research question and which set of research skills you master, it will be necessary to have some understanding of measurement-based and statistically analysed research. Very few areas of educational and social science research are completely devoid of applications in this area and consequently when engaging in background reading, you will inevitably encounter articles or papers that report the use of a measurement instrument and maybe even employ some statistical analysis. When reading such papers, it is desirable not only to understand the point the author is trying to make and defend, but also to begin to be able to evaluate any claims. This is usually not a simple matter of either accepting or rejecting the study, but assigning a relative value to the claims made, based on the quality of the research. The question of quality of research is confounded by the fact that some shortcomings of published work will simply be attributable to poor writing style as opposed to inappropriate research design or faulty procedure. One must assume that in the professional research world Disraeli's view that 'There are three kinds of lies: lies, damned lies, and statistics' (Huff, 1954) is not necessarily true, and should probably be changed to 'There are lies, damned lies, and distorted or poorly presented statistics.' Your skill in identifying the latter should be enhanced through critical reading and practice in evaluating research papers.

On the other hand, one must not be fooled into thinking that just because there are numbers to support the results that the results are 'the truth'. With statistical studies, the answer is more accurately 'probably the truth'. In the past, there have been overly optimistic expectations of statistically based research, which when the reality became apparent, led to a decline in interest in the approach (Campbell and Stanley, 1963). Answers in social science research are no easier to come by (and usually harder, considering what is being studied) than answers in any other discipline, be it science, humanities or art.

How critical one is of any research will often depend on how the results are to be used. If decisions are to be made that are a matter of life and death (say, the use of a new drug), then the reader is very critical of the process of arriving at the results. But if you are interested only from the viewpoint of looking at possible variables to study in your own research, then you are really looking for clues and quite reasonably will be less critical. In any case, it is best to be able to evaluate what you have read and not accept everything blindly or, at the other extreme, ignore it.

A key aspect to evaluating statistics-based research is to realize that to justify adequately one's results, a researcher must have followed the rules and met the underlying assumptions; failure to do so can cast doubt on any claims or completely invalidate them. To check this requires some understanding of what is involved in carrying out this type of research. The objective of this book is not to prepare you to go out and do research, but to provide you with sufficient insight into the problems a researcher faces to evaluate research. To carry out this type of research successfully requires numerous additional skills that are the subject of other books. This is not intended to discourage, but to warn you that statistically based research requires care and skill if it is to produce acceptable (valid and reliable) results. Too often in the past, potential researchers have arrived at the computer centre, clutching piles of data asking, 'what do I do with it?' Without careful planning at all stages, the results produced by the computer will follow the old computer saying 'garbage in, garbage out'. The First Law of Social Science Research should be:

> No amount of massaging by a computer-based statistical
> package will rescue a poorly planned research project.

Having made that point, let us return to the overall question of evaluating research reports, *some* of which will use statistics.

Criteria for evaluating research

Wallace (1978) provides a comprehensive two-dimensional model of the scientific process that illustrates the complexity of the process as part of theory-building (Figure 1.2). The paths from the rectangular box containing the *hypotheses* to the one with the *theories* pass through boxes and ovals which are the sources of strength or weakness of the support for those theories. Consequently, the support for the theories will only be maintained by the validity and appropriateness of the methodological processes summarized in the ovals and subsequent logical consistency of the information generated in the boxes. Since we will concentrate on evaluating research reports, a simpler, more linear model will be used to facilitate the learning process, but one that includes evaluating all the processes contained in Wallace's model. Note that his more complete model

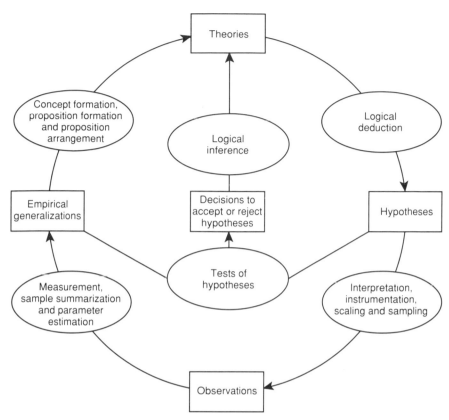

Figure 1.2   *The principal informational components (rectangles), methodological controls (ovals) and information transformations (arrows) of the scientific process (Wallace, 1978). Reprinted with permission from: Wallace, Walter L.* The Logic of Science in Sociology. *(New York: Aldine de Gruyter) Copyright © 1971 Walter L. Wallace.*

primarily elaborates on the activities in the bottom half of the simple model of Figure 1.1. Above the line is the rationale for any research, a process all researchers will engage in when designing a project.

Let us begin by extending the process outlined in Figure 1.1. to include the kinds of processes suggested by Wallace, but in a more linear structure. Assuming that the research questions designated by the researcher indicate a need for the measurement of variables and possibly the use of statistical analysis, a linear version of the process will be something like that shown in Figure 1.3, with additional detail shown below the dashed line.

In order to evaluate research, a condensed set of criteria has been identified and set up as a Profiling Sheet (a complete version is provided at the end of this book). These criteria will serve as guides for evaluating studies and summarize the more extensive criteria introduced below and elaborated on in subsequent chapters. You should be proficient in using the Profiling Sheet as an evaluation tool by the end of this course of study.

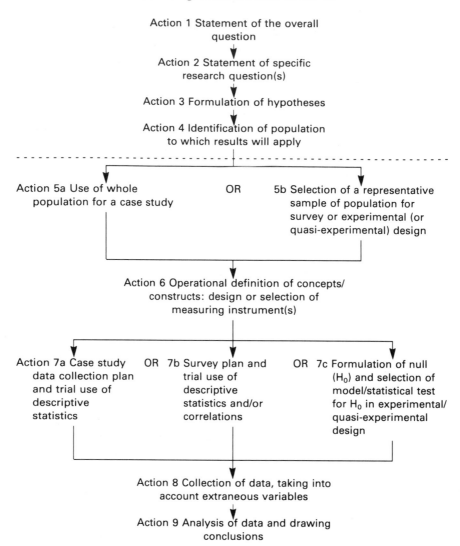

Figure 1.3 *Summary of the processes of designing and carrying out measurement-based studies: experimental/quasi-experimental, survey and case study.*

This sheet will be used in Activities that will involve you in evaluating a variety of research papers, including those of your own choice. The 'Action' numbers in brackets under the column headings of the Profiling Sheet are common to those in Figure 1.3 and the numbered paragraphs below, to help you to link the evaluation process with the overall research design process. Also, each column is dealt with in greater detail in a subsequent chapter. The following paragraphs start at the bottom of Figure 1.3, with Action 9, since it is the conclusions that are of prime interest.

How the validity of these depends on the whole design will become more apparent as the analysis proceeds back up through the chart. The Profiling Sheet may be photocopied for future use in evaluating research papers.

To understand the interrelations of each action taken in the linear model used here, the discussion will start from the bottom of Figure 1.3 and work upwards. This way, it will be possible to take the results and claims made by a researcher and see how strongly they are justified. The brief discussion below is intended to provide an overview of research planning to put the whole practice into some perspective. Each column will be fully covered in later chapters, as indicated by each Action summarized below.

Action 9. Analyse data and draw conclusions (Chapters 6, 7 and 8)

Some conclusions verge upon blatant speculation, while others tend to be overly conservative. While there are some studies that make outrageous claims, the main criticism is usually not whether the conclusion is right or wrong, but the strength of the support provided, which includes how well the researcher has justified the conclusions. Very little in human behaviour and activity can be predicted exactly, so most studies are looking for evidence of trends or tendencies, rather than absolute cause and effect events. No matter what the findings may seem to prove, there are always exceptions. Therefore, when reading reports of studies, one looks not only for claims of relative confidence in a conclusion, but also for supporting evidence. Much of the latter will be found (or not found, as the case may be) in decisions and processes in the other eight Actions that precede the conclusions in the report. The strength of the conclusions is no stronger than the relative level of rigour with which the other steps are executed, as will be seen.

One type of outcome does merit special consideration. Statements often appear in statistically based reports such that there was a *significant* difference between the scores of two groups. This is often used to justify the existence of a cause and effect relationship between two variables. What is meant by statistically significant? It simply means that *it did not occur by chance alone*, there is probably some external cause. For example, the IQ test scores of two identical groups of children are found to be 'significantly different'. This means the difference is so great that it is probably not a chance occurrence and is not due to the natural variation in IQ test scores in the population. It does not *prove* that the variables being investigated caused the difference, it only says that the difference exists and is probably not just a random occurrence. It is up to the researcher to prove that the variables under consideration are the actual cause and eliminate the possibility of any other variable(s) contributing to the results found.

What you must check as a reader of research is how well the researcher has accounted for all the other possible causes and how well he or she has justified the identification of the cause of the observed effect, if this is the case. When a report omits a discussion on this, then the reader begins to wonder about the quality of the research. Later discussion in Chapter 8 will point up some subtle and not so subtle potential sources of faulty conclusions. In addition, a conscientious researcher will make recommendations and identify limitations of the study, mainly in terms of implications for practitioners and other researchers who might make decisions on the basis of the study.

Finally, there are situations where the use of statistical tests is not even appropriate. Just because there are numerical data does not mean that it is necessary or justified to carry out statistical tests on them. The most common situation where statistical tests are inappropriate is when the whole population is used. *Inferential statistics*, which is the formal name for the study of such tests, assume you have a representative sample of the whole population. Inferences about the whole population are made on the basis of the sample through the statistical tests. Thus, if the whole population is used, for example in a case study, inferential statistics are inappropriate. Later, in Chapters 6 and 7, we will consider criteria for the appropriate use of inferential statistics, without having to consider specific statistical tests.

Action 8. Collecting data (controlling variables) (Chapter 8)

One might be tempted to think that this is a straightforward process, but there can be many problems. In addition to those associated directly with how the data are actually collected, ranging from the wording of covering letters for questionnaires to the interpersonal skills of an interviewer, there are other sources. A prime one may be the measuring instrument itself, like a test, questionnaire or observation schedule, which will be discussed under Action 6. The sampling procedure (Action 5) will also affect how effectively this step is carried out, as will one's choice of statistics (Action 7.)

Any report should describe the data collection procedure in sufficient detail so as to allow the reader to judge its appropriateness. Ideally, there would be enough detail to allow another researcher to replicate the study, something that happens all too rarely. In most disciplines, before the results of a study (especially a statistically based one) are widely accepted and acted on, the procedure must be replicated. For reasons that are probably associated with the dictum that all research *must* be something 'new', this tends to be unfashionable in the social sciences. If the guiding principle was truly that research should reflect some originality as stated by most institutions of higher education, then replication would constitute a part of the evaluation of a research methodology. Research does not have to be new to demand considerable original thought in planning and execution.

Action 7a. Plan case study data collection and use of descriptive statistics (Chapter 5)

Going into a situation without a plan, intending only to observe whatever happens with no strategy as to what to look for, has been shown to be a good recipe for disaster. A researcher needs to prepare for the data collection, the exact nature of the preparation depending on the type of study. For example, to conduct an interview, questions must be prepared (Action 6) and tried out, recording systems (paper and pencil as well as electronic) devised, date arranged with subjects etc. Observation in classrooms requires an observation schedule, a list of categories of events to look for related to the concepts being investigated. Failure to carry out such preparation is often the source of problems that manifest themselves at other stages. Even a decision made before collecting data on just how it will be presented can point up omissions as well as superfluous data. While journal articles often report only the salient parts of data collection, research reports can reveal the problem of poor planning and resultant weak data.

Action 7b. Plan survey and use of descriptive statistics and/or correlations (Chapters 5 and 6)

The design of the questionnaire or measuring device is the focus of Action 6; by trying it out before distribution the researcher can avoid oversights. Deciding on what descriptive statistics will be used (graphs, charts etc.) and what correlations will be calculated *before* collecting data can help in identifying omissions as well as superfluous requests for data. This may seem unnecessary, but failure to do so has resulted in attempts to measure too many variables and contributed to overly long questionnaires which in turn have affected whether the recipient was willing to complete the form. This in turn has affected whether a sample was considered representative of a larger population, or just volunteers and therefore of questionable representativeness.

Action 7c. Formulate null hypothesis and select statistical model/ test (Chapters 6 and 7)

The *null hypothesis* is just a way of stating the expected outcome of the research in terms of the statistical model used. Such a statement basically says that no statistically significant difference is expected to be found, for example, between (among) groups or that a correlation found is not different from one found by chance alone. Statistical significance, though, is no guarantee of educational, sociological or psychological significance. But let us be optimistic and consider a study that has the general hypothesis that one set of learning material is more effective than another. The researcher might state it as a null hypothesis:

There will be no significant difference in improvement of

performance by the two groups using the two different sets of learning materials.

Having selected two representative groups of students to try the materials, the researchers would then look at the difference between pre- and post-test scores (gain scores: one possible measure of learning) and compare the scores of the two groups. If the test showed that there was a statistically significant difference in gain scores, then the null hypothesis would be 'rejected'. All that the researchers know is that the difference probably did not occur by chance alone. It would still be up to them to justify that the superior nature of one set of material over the other was the sole cause of the difference observed (not necessarily a trivial task). Such experimental designs were originally developed by researchers in biological disciplines, but have been found to be of value in some situations in social science research.

Stating a null hypothesis tends to compel the researcher to think what the statistical test is *really* going to tell him or her. Occasionally, null hypotheses are stated in a form to suggest that there is no cause and effect relationship, thus a significant statistical result rejecting this would confirm the causal relationship. This is an improper use of statistics. Remember, rejecting a null hypothesis only indicates that whatever has happened very probably did not happen by chance alone. Assuming the truth of this, it is still up to the researcher to justify the cause by ensuring nothing else could have possibly caused it.

The criteria for selecting an appropriate statistical model and test are numerous and complex because of the diversity of tests available. But any report ought to justify the choice of statistical tests for the questions to be answered. Some guidance will be provided in Chapter 7, but you may have to consult experts or refer to texts on the subject of statistical research design to begin to resolve completely the detailed question of appropriateness.

All the points about measurement, data collection, sampling and interpretation of statistical significance must be considered when evaluating a report. One supposed advantage of selecting research reports from refereed journals is that the selection process has prevented reports of poorly conducted studies from being published, though as one might expect this is not a perfect process.

Action 6. Measuring instruments as operational definitions
(Chapter 4)

Most research studies in the social sciences involve rather abstract concepts or constructs devised by the researcher or other members of the discipline, like intelligence, wealth, class, social mobility, knowledge of a language. This means that to investigate a problem based on an abstract idea, a way of measuring that idea is going to be required. This will mean devising or selecting a measuring 'instrument' that will constitute an operational (observable) definition of this abstraction. The best known example is that of intelligence, something that we all talk about but cannot observe directly. Often impressions are formed of someone's relative intelligence based on observations, but a more objective process is needed in many situations. Consequently, over the years, several IQ (intelligence quotient) tests have been devised that purport to reflect objectively a person's intelligence. But there are arguments as to what constitutes intelligence and, therefore, what should be included in the test. There have been discussions focusing on such undesirable influences on given tests such as a single culture, what constitutes language, and sex bias. These leave the reader in a difficult position as to knowing whether any test used was a valid test of intelligence for the study under consideration.

But this is not the only problem. What if an appropriate test does not already exist? To create a measuring instrument requires another set of skills, time to develop the test, and persons to try them out before they are used in the research project. The reliability and validity of researcher-designed tests can be suspect, though often an indication and justification of these are provided in the research report for the reader's perusal.

In addition, when evaluating a study, a researcher should look for logical consistency across the original question, the constructs/concepts from the theory applied and the measuring instruments used as the operational definition. A sound underlying theory and references to previous work lends credibility to any study. It is not necessary to have earth-shaking discoveries or to create new theories in a study to make a useful contribution to the realm of research. Most studies are built on the work of others; research tends to progress in small steps, not huge leaps.

Actions 4 and 5. The population and selecting a representative sample (Chapter 3)

In a statistically based study, the group(s) chosen to participate in a study tend to be one of the following:

- a whole population,
- a randomly selected sample from a population,
- a purposively selected sample from a population,
- volunteers,
- an unspecified group.

The further one goes down the list, the less representative a group is of a larger population. Rarely is it possible to use a whole population of a worthwhile size, consequently samples are taken and inferences made about the whole population based on the sample (recall the term inferential statistics). Also, it is possible to find a combination of the above five levels. For example, it is possible to have randomly selected a sample to participate in an activity, but not all those selected agree to do so. While the original sample was randomly selected (very desirable), the resulting study was carried out by volunteers. In such cases, to strengthen his or her case, a researcher would have to ascertain why some chose not to participate, to assure the reader that it was not for reasons pertaining to the research (offended by a questionnaire, afraid to do a test). Any study using volunteers should address itself to the question of why some did and others did not volunteer. Obviously, the further up the list a study is, the stronger the generalizability of the results. In summary, the way a sample is selected affects how strongly a researcher can justify the generalizability of a study.

Action 3. Formulation of hypotheses (Chapter 2)

As noted at the beginning of this chapter, stating the expected outcome of a study (hypothesizing) tends to focus the researcher's attention on relevant problems and inform the reader of the purpose of the study. If the research does not use inferential statistics, then a general statement is quite acceptable, whereas the use of inferential statistics really requires a null hypothesis.

Actions 1 and 2. Statement of general and specific research questions (Chapter 2)

These do not have to be in any formal terms, but should be supported by a rationale for the study that includes references to relevant models, theories and previous studies. A general statement of the area of research should be followed by some indication of what specific research question the report is addressing itself to. Articles that describe the process involved in data collection, the measurement instruments, statistical tests and conclusions without indicating the reason for it all may describe research that lacked direction, or may just be poorly reported.

Evaluating the report of a study

To ensure the validity of claims and reliability (replicability) of their work, researchers need to adhere to the kinds of guidelines outlined above. Limitations of resources, the fickleness of subjects and just plain bad luck, to name a few, can reduce the strength and generalizability of results of a study. The more complex a process such as this, the more places things can go wrong.

Obviously, the results of this type of evaluation are going to depend not only on the quality of the research, but also on the comprehensiveness of the written report. Writing about research is not an easy task, especially when it is done for a journal that has limitations on the length of articles. Such constraints can affect writing style and contribute to the omission of essential information that would facilitate the evaluation of the study. Thus, the process of evaluating a research report will reflect not only the quality of the research, but the quality of the report, since any report should provide the reader with sufficient information to assess the quality of the study, or ideally even replicate it. In some disciplines, this last criterion is most important.

As can be seen from the previous sections and the Profiling Sheet that will serve as a guide to evaluation, a reader expects to find certain types of information about the implementation of a study, as well as the results. The following list summarizes what might be considered the essential components of even a short report or journal article describing a research project, though not necessarily presented in this order:

- Clear statement of research question and hypotheses, supported by literature references.
- Description of the subjects, and if a sample, the population to whom the results are to apply.
- Description of the measuring instrument(s), with some indication of validity and reliability.
- An account of (typically) the conditions under which the data were collected.
- Presentation of the results, graphically where appropriate.
- Summary of statistical analysis, with clear indication of why the specific test(s) were chosen.
- A statement of the conclusions with limitations, and recommendations for further research.

The evaluation of a report will involve determining sins of omission as well as sins of commission, and consequently there will be occasions when the lack of information is more frustrating than being able to identify poor procedure. While a full report may provide sufficient detail to allow the replication of a study, most journal articles have such length restrictions placed upon them that this is not possible. There is nothing to prevent the reader from contacting the author of a journal article and asking for greater detail.

A problem of rigour

With so many possible pitfalls, how does anyone ever produce decent research? While the task is complex, it is not impossible and is based upon a long tradition of skill development. It is desirable to take a scientific approach, which includes an eclectic view towards data collecting approaches, encompassing case studies, experimental and survey research, all complementing each other where appropriate. Carried out with intellectual honesty and with adequate skills, endeavours that depend upon the systematic observation of people are more likely to contribute to the advancement of understanding the human condition than those that depend upon eloquence of argument. Such an approach maintains that to understand where we are going, we must know where we are. One overall criterion for the quality of a study is the relative potential to replicate the process with a different group or sample, and arrive at much the same conclusions, regardless of the paradigm employed.

What skills do such approaches demand? These do not consist of the easily identifiable ones associated with the natural sciences, such as measuring weight or assembling apparatus, but they are skills that all scientists possess none the less. In order to investigate exactly what these are, let us first engage in a bit of fun. Please carry out Activity 1.1 *before* reading any further.

Activity 1.1

This exercise will illustrate some of the problems facing a researcher. Take a candle (large or small, it makes no difference), and make a list of 30 of its characteristics. You can do anything you like to it (e.g. light it, throw it, drop it in water.) Restrict your list to about 30 items, otherwise you can go on forever. Set the list aside for a while; it will be used in Activity 1.2.

Process skills of social science research

While one usually associates the content of such subjects as biology, chemistry and physics with the word 'science', it is more realistic to think of this word as describing a set of *intellectual processes*. Many of these we all acquire with maturity as part of life's survival skills, but some need special training and all can be applied to investigations in social science as well as the natural sciences. A useful scheme for isolating these is the set of thirteen 'process skills' produced by the American Association for the Advancement of Science (AAAS) in the 1960s, which are closely related to goals and aims defined by the Science 5–13 project in the UK and other international science curriculum development projects (Lockard, 1980). These were defined in an effort to encourage science teachers to consider science as more than a set of facts, and to treat science more appropriately as a verb rather than a noun. The aim of all of these projects was to develop enquiring minds and a scientific approach to problem-solving, one that should extend to social science research as well. Not surprisingly, this implies that any scientific discipline is not going to be static, but dynamic.

Below are a set of suggested *social science process skills*, based on the above two schemes. The order (slightly different from the originals) is hierarchical, each process being a higher level skill than the one before it. As you progress through this book, you will be given opportunities to evaluate the possession of these skills by researchers who publish their work.

1 Observation Events occur round us all the time, some of which we notice and others we do not. Observing is selective, we see what we try to see, otherwise ours senses would be overwhelmed. In social science research, there is some necessity to be trained as an observer, since some of the events that need to be observed and recorded are so common as not to seem significant to the untrained. For example, to study the use of positive reinforcement in a classroom may require a researcher to count up how often it is used within a lesson. This may require knowing what the children perceive of as reinforcement and watching the classroom interaction carefully. Whether the reinforcement is effective may be a separate question.

2 Event/time relations This involves investigations that are time-dependent, for example, where frequency of an event may be important. This may result in considering rates of occurrence, sometimes over relatively short periods (minutes) and for other studies over relatively long periods (months, years). For example, if one were investigating alcoholism, there is considerable difference between subjects who consume half a litre of whisky in an evening and those who take a month to consume the same amount. The rate of consumption would be of more interest than the amount.

3 Communication It is often assumed that educated adults can communicate, at least in writing. But there is considerable difference in writing a letter to a friend, an essay or a novel, and writing a research report. Many studies fail to communicate essential aspects of the process, leaving the reader wondering if the conclusions were really justified.

4 Prediction An intelligent guess, extrapolation or interpolation ultimately may be the source of a question that will be the basis of a research project. A 'What if . . .?' question can stimulate speculation that only becomes accepted fact if followed by an investigation to answer it.

5 Classification We all classify objects and events as a way of bringing order to observations. Some schemes have relatively wide acceptance, like physical characteristics, professions, cognitive level of questions on a test, while others generate considerable discussion, such as social class. Devising a classification scheme can be a very complex task that may involve creating new concepts, isolating characteristics into which persons or events can be categorized and/or operationally defining (see 9 below) abstract concepts. In any case, the defining of mutually exclusive categories that can be used effectively by researchers is not a trivial task.

6 Inference Distinguishing between observation and inference is not always easy. An inference is a subjective explanation of an observation. One may observe the wick sticking out of each end of a candle and infer that it is a single string going through the candle, but this is not the only possible inference. Further investigations would be necessary to be sure. Observing a teacher praise a child for an answer in class and the child subsequently smiling, you may infer that the child is encouraged. Alternatively, the child could be smiling for other reasons (a giggle in the class, a sign of relief, an embarrassed smile, a smile of self-satisfaction for getting it correct). Resolving conflicting inferences in human situations is much more difficult than deciding which is most accurate in material ones like the candle. This makes the choice of what to observe even more difficult, since to resolve conflicting inferences may require multiple observations.

7 Number relations   Quantified data can be more meaningfully presented and analysed in tabular and graphical form. Some statistical tests will help to resolve issues after the data have been collected in a way which would not otherwise be possible. For example, a correlation coefficient may not mean as much to some people as the scatter diagram from which it is derived. Selecting the most appropriate mathematical tool will often help in conveying one's results.

8 Measurement   In a physical sense, measurement means using instruments like rulers and balances. Here we shall take it to mean designing and using measuring instruments like tests, questionnaires and interview schedules. There is a considerable technology associated with the design of these, covered extensively in other texts, but some of their main characteristics will be considered in Chapter 4.

9 Making operational definitions   As noted with respect to Action 6 in Figure 1.3, most concepts that tend to be investigated in the social sciences are abstract. This means that there is a necessity to select or devise an observable activity that is indicative of the concept. For example, a score on an IQ test is an operational definition of intelligence. There is no direct, physiological way of measuring intelligence; thus, if this concept is to be used as part of an investigation, then an indirect means must be found. Income and educational background may be factors that are used to determine social class. The relative validity of an operational definition may well be dependent upon the possession of measurement skills (see 8 above) and/or the ability to make sound inferences (see 6 above).

10 Formulating hypotheses   A hypothesis is an educated guess, an expectation. It may suggest a causal relationship, but not necessarily. Whatever the hypothesis, the aim is to test it in some way to see if it is supported or not. Formulating a hypothesis is not an easy skill and one too often neglected by researchers who leap into a study without the adequately defined reason that every investigation needs. A formal statement often compels a researcher to resolve issues that a more woolly statement or question can hide. The whole design of a research study will be affected by a hypothesis, thus it is better to establish one early before too much intellectual effort is invested in a dead end. This process will highlight the need for clear operational definitions and sound concepts, as well as the need to clarify how variables will be identified and controlled (see 12 below).

11 Interpreting data   Data appear in many forms, some numerical, some transcripts of interviews. Raw data have little meaning and must be turned into understandable information. Numbers and statistical results by themselves are of little interest and difficult to make any sense of. What does it mean to have a correlation of 0.45? It is not easy for a reader to understand the significance of a graph on its own. For example, does the shape of a histogram of scores make any difference in a study? Something can be statistically significant without, for example, being educationally significant. What does a statistical significance level of 0.05 tell us in a specific case? A researcher's ability to interpret the data collected in a logically consistent manner without making unwarranted claims or under-rating the strength of the findings is an essential skill.

12 Identifying and controlling variables   This is a difficult enough task in the physical and biological sciences, where the experimenter has a reasonable amount of control of the environment. In the social sciences, it is even more difficult. Just being able to identify variables in a social interaction requires considerable perception, and is related to other earlier skills. For example, what causes a 'discipline problem' in a classroom? The pupil's behaviour? Provocation by the teacher? Domestic (home) problems on either side leaving one party short-tempered?

To control variables can be even more difficult. For example, an investigation into the effectiveness of a set of learning materials has little or no control over what the children do outside class or what they see on television at home. If some effect is observed, it is up to the researcher to justify that this was the result of a specific variable, which is usually achieved through the careful design of the investigation (see 13 below).

13 Designing an investigation   This is the integration of all the above skills in the design of an investigation that will collect data and ultimately provide meaningful information. The design will take into account problems of determining the question and hypothesis, of defining, controlling and measuring/observing variables, and of interpreting results and communicating. A well-planned study is done with considerable foresight so that in the final report, few excuses are made for flaws and the results are justifiable *and* educationally or socially significant.

Having considered this list of process skills, let us return to the data you collected on the candle and carry out Activity 1.2 (p. 22).

Activity 1.2

Take your list from Activity 1.1 and classify each item as one of the 13 Process Skills and consider the following question:

1 How many of them were something other than observations?
2 For those that were inferences, do you think your fellow researchers would agree with you? Would they have others? Compare notes.
3 Compare those you classify as 'observations' with those of fellow researchers. Does everyone have the same ones? How could you assure that another group observed the important characteristics? What would constitute being 'important'?
4 You have carried out a detailed study of one candle, a 'case study'. Outline briefly how you would extend this into a survey of a variety of candles to see if they possess the same characteristics.
5 If you take a candle, light it and then turn an empty tumbler upside down over it, the candle will burn for a while and extinguish. Briefly describe a plan for an experimental study to determine if there is a difference in post-covering burning time for candles of different colours.

Investigating objects is much easier than investigating people and their traits. The difficulty in all the skills applied to social science research lies in the variability and complexity of people. As noted earlier, objective measurement depends upon the operational definition stemming from an abstract concept described in the hypothesis. You could begin a list of characteristics of social science research that makes it more difficult and challenging than natural science research, and add to it as you progress through the text and its exercises. But first carry out Activity 1.3.

Activity 1.3

Select and read carefully an article describing a research project in an area of interest to you. Note occurrences of the employment of as many of the Process Skills as you can.

Summary

In this chapter, a rough outline of the major Actions in designing research has been presented as a foundation for building a set of identifiable procedures that can be used to evaluate research reports. Each of these Actions has been briefly described and the following chapters will elaborate on the criteria for judging the quality of execution of each. These criteria are summarized on the Profiling Sheet, a full copy of which is provided at the end of Chapter 8. The overall aim is to provide you with the opportunity to apply these criteria to articles and reports, providing practice in evaluating research.

Also, this first chapter has introduced a set of Process Skills for social science, which researchers tend to employ when carrying out all the Actions. The level of acquisition of these will be much more difficult to infer from reports and journal articles, but they should help in identifying the sources of both good and poor practice in research.

It is recognized that the models and skills presented here are not definitive and necessarily widely accepted. What is of primary importance is to provide the reader with a basic set of criteria to begin to evaluate research reports. You are encouraged to develop your own model, refining skill sets to suit your area(s) of research, as experience dictates. The only real sin is *not* to have any criteria by which to judge the quality of research reports.

References

Blum, M.L. and Foos, P.W. (1986) *Data Gathering: Experimental Methods Plus*. Harper & Row.

Campbell, D.T. and Stanley, J.C. (1963) *Experimental and Quasi-experimental Designs for Research*. Rand McNally.

Cohen, L. and Manion, L. (1989) *Research Methods in Education*, 3rd edn. Routledge.

Huff, D. (1954) *How to Lie with Statistics*. Penguin.

Kerlinger, F.N. (1986) *Foundations of Behavioral Research*, 3rd edn. Holt, Rinehart & Winston.

Lockard, J.D. (1980) *UNESCO Handbook for Science Teachers*. Heinemann.

Nisbet, J. and Watt, J. (1978) *Case Study* (Rediguide 26). University of Nottingham.

Wallace, W. (1978) 'An overview of elements in the scientific process'. in J. Bynner and K.M. Stribley (eds) *Social Research: Principles and Procedures*. Longman. pp.4–10.

2

Questions and Hypotheses

'Good morning,' said Deep Thought.

'Er . . . Good morning, O Deep Thought,' said Loonquawl nervously, 'do you have . . . er, that is . . .'

'An answer for you?' interrupted Deep Thought majestically. 'Yes. I have.'

The two men shivered with expectancy. Their waiting had not been in vain.

'There really is one?' breathed Phouchg.

'There really is one,' confirmed Deep Thought.

'To Everything? To the great Question of Life, the Universe and Everything?'

'Yes.'

Both of the men had been trained for this moment, their lives had been preparation for it, they had been selected at birth as those who would witness the answer, but even so they found themselves gasping and squirming like excited children.

'And you're ready to give it to us?' urged Loonquawl.

'I am.'

'Now?'

'Now,' said Deep Thought.

They both licked their dry lips.

'Though I don't think,' added Deep Thought, 'that you're going to like it.'

'Doesn't matter!' said Phouchg. 'We must know it! Now!'

'Now?' inquired Deep Thought.

'Yes! Now . . .'

'Alright,' said the computer and settled into silence again. The two men fidgeted. The tension was unbearable.

'You're not going to like it,' observed Deep Thought.

'Tell us!'

'Alright,' said Deep Thought. 'The Answer to the Great Question . . .'

'Yes . . .'

'Is . . .' said Deep Thought, and paused.

'Yes . . .!'

'Is . . .'

'Yes . . . !!! . . .?'

'Forty-two,' said Deep Thought, with infinite majesty and calm.

(Adams, 1979)

Typically, researchers would like to tackle significant problems and find meaningful answers. The most difficult part of starting a research project is often that of identifying the best question to ask, one that is meaningful, whose answer contributes to the discipline, and whose resulting research can be carried out within the resources available. But even with unlimited resources, one has to be careful about the original guiding question, as Adams so aptly indicates above, because even after seven and a half million years of thinking, Deep Thought's answer was still difficult to fathom.

Before considering what constitutes a sound research question and good hypotheses, it is worthwhile examining their role in the research process. First, there is the difficulty of vocabulary, including words like 'hypothesis' and 'theory'. Terminology often gets in the way of understanding, particularly when technical terms assume common everyday meaning and usage. It is not my intention to delve into a discussion of a philosophy of science applied to social science, but some clarification should prove useful and further reading can be pursued in such texts as Blum and Foos (1986). A simplified definition based upon their work will suffice: *scientific theories* should be considered as explanations of how things function or why events occur. These are based upon discoveries and data collection resulting in tested *hypotheses*, which can be considered to be proposed relations and expectations. Theories are presented to explain facts (correctly or wrongly) but are not facts themselves. They are not absolute answers and are continually subject to new, often conflicting, hypotheses. While sometimes these result in refuting an existing theory, more often the result is a refinement of the explanation which enhances the power of prediction when applying them.

Blum and Foos (1986) are quite adamant that explanations are not in their own right theories. There are explanations that are the result of *rationalism*, based upon reason alone (some of it faulty) and not backed by systematic observation. This can result in almost trite responses to complex problems, such as why are there so many out of work? Saying that it is because of unemployment only provides a label, not an explanation. There are rationalisms that do provide correct explanations and those that do not, but the best description is that of 'dataless reasoning'. It is often heard as the explanation given for some event by journalists during television news broadcasts: 'Why has the value of the pound dropped today?' The quick answer may be something like 'There has been panic buying of other currencies due to a drop in interest rates.' Has the reporter actually asked even a sample of currency speculators why they have traded today? Not usually. Rationalisms may be a starting point for formulating a research question or hypothesis, but are unlikely to stand up to scrutiny for long.

Questions

Research questions that are too vague do not provide sufficient direction for the research effort. This happens all too often with committees set up to investigate such grandiose topics as Mathematics Teaching or The English Language as Learned in Schools, or The Cause of Poverty. Rarely is everyone satisfied with the answers. While a researcher may wish to contribute to the answer of a global question, the actual project needs to be guided by a more specific question or set of specific questions.

Most published research in journals tends to result from reasonable limited statements of research intent. Yet even these can tend to be vague, poorly stated or not even presented at all. The poorly stated ones are often followed by research without direction, producing results that are inconclusive, or projects that generate vast amounts of data followed by attempts to make some sense of it (the consequences of data snooping, fishing and hunting will be discussed later in the chapter). In addition to answering questions directly with definitive conclusions, one of the functions of research is to eliminate alternative explanations or false theories (Popper, 1978). If the original question or hypothesis is weakly stated, then it is much easier to ignore evidence that contradicts the research team's, and there is the danger that they will find what they want to find.

While Popper (1978) feels that the source of a research question is the personal business of the researcher, most statements of research questions are supported by literature citations of previously conducted studies. In particular, Greer (1978) suggests three general categories of research problems in the social sciences:

1 *Policy problems* that stem from society's values related to poverty, mental health, race relations and crime. These tend to result from a perceived discrepancy between what is considered to be the ideal and the actual situation. This often results in abstract constructs of complex social functions, with a focus on how to achieve some effect or social change.
2 *Social philosophy*, intellectual problems stemming from the conflict between established ideologies and contemporary events. For example, the study of Marxism leads to the serious consideration of class in society. The aim is to integrate new ideas into established schemas.
3 *Previously accumulated propositions*, which become the starting points for establishing more comprehensive theories or models. Positive reinforcement may be of prime interest to the classroom teacher, but the educational psychologist will be more concerned with its role in a general learning theory. The problems tend to be of broader interest to the discipline, though to the casual observer this may not always be apparent. Sometimes it is more difficult to see the relevance of a specific study to a specific model or theory. This can be due to a combination of the perceived need for building on existing theories, collected evidence, and structures of the discipline, exacerbated by the rigour required to resolve an individual problem.

All three areas could generate studies that require the collection of data to resolve issues. In each, a clear statement of the question as well as its links with established thinking (though not necessarily agreement) is essential in the reporting of a study.

Some research questions might be considered to originate from more than one source or a conflict between two. Educational decisions can raise public issues that can transcend the categories, such as the desirability of bussing children to schools to maintain a racial balance, and the need for basic skills such as spelling and multiplication tables in school in the era of calculators and spell-check facilities on computers. Before going further, please consider Activity 2.1.

Activity 2.1

Below are three statements of research questions. Suggest and justify what you think the origin of each is from one or more of: policy problems, social philosophy, and/or previously accumulated propositions:

(a) Is intelligence determined by heredity or environment?
(b) What is the relationship between crime rate and levels of unemployment?
(c) Why do many people prefer to go on highly structured holidays (pre-booked hotels, guided tours, planned events) rather than self-organized ones?

How can the reader of research reports begin to evaluate the quality of a research question? Kerlinger (1986) maintains that there are three criteria for good problem statements in the form of questions. The statement should

- express a relationship between variables,
- be stated in unambiguous terms in question form, and
- should imply the possibility of empirical testing.

The last criterion recognizes that there are valid philosophical and theological questions to be answered, but these are not in the realm of research covered in this text. This still leaves a problem for the reader when reading a report or article as to deciding the adequacy of a research question. A question could meet all of the above criteria and still be unacceptable. Before considering other issues related to the statement of a research question, carry out Activity 2.2 (p. 28).

Activity 2.2

Below are three statements of research questions (the first two are adapted from Kerlinger, 1986). Read each in turn, considering its merits then pass judgement on its quality *before* reading the model answers at the end of this chapter. Since these statements are taken out of context, you may disagree with the evaluation supplied, which is quite reasonable assuming you can defend yours.

(a)   Does democratic education improve the learning of children?
(b)   Do encouraging comments by the teacher enhance student performance?
(c)   Is it best to provide financial assistance to the unemployed?

You may have found the task in Activity 2.2 an awkward one, since the questions were presented in isolation. Most reports will provide a reasonable rationale supported by other research, presented in the form of references to published reports and journal articles. Occasionally, a reader will find a question that lacks such intellectual backing, leaving the feeling that the statement lacks sufficient support and justification. In some cases, the question is based solely upon belief, unsupported by previous research. While this is not unheard of, nor totally unreasonable, it is unlikely that a research report will have its basic question unsupported by other research. Even those proposing a radical stance will cite the literature to which it is opposed.

A second reason for expecting a justification for the research question is that the writer ought to be educating his readers and promoting further enquiry. Social science research rarely generates questions that involve totally isolated variables, and for the sake of the readership, the author ought to be drawing on the experience of others and encouraging the expansion of interest and effort in that area. Relevant articles have been skipped over by readers because the author has not stated the question unambiguously or presented a sound case for investigating it early in the discussion.

Hypotheses

As noted earlier, hypotheses as presented in a report or study are a more formal means of stating research intent, more firmly fixing the direction of a study. These will have a direct influence on the eventual choice of operational definition(s) of concepts and constructs, which will be the measuring instrument(s) used to collect the data, as will be seen in Chapter 3. This need to consider stages of research out of the order described earlier simply points up the somewhat artificial nature of the linear model of research design chosen in Chapter 1, since a researcher will most likely consider these together. It does not negate the need for a statement of a hypothesis early in a report, nor the desirability of a researcher establishing a hypothesis that is acceptable early in the study. Kerlinger (1986) notes 'After intellectualising the problem, after turning back on experience for possible solutions, after observing relevant phenomena, the scientist may formulate a hypothesis. A hypothesis is a conjectural statement, a tentative proposition, about the relationship between two or more variables.'

'Observing relevant phenomena' may include surveying the literature and referring to the experiences of others, as well as first-hand observation.

Popper (1978) maintains the need for hypotheses as part of social science research on the basis that such endeavour tends to be deductive, with a statement of hypothesis followed by systematically determining the fallacy of competing answers. He maintains that while we use knowledge of ourselves to make statements about others or people in general, these are hypotheses that must be tested. Take, for example, the following statements: 'A friend of mine buys all his marijuana from this accountant. You know all these accountants deal in drugs on the side. How else could they be so rich?' Substitute for 'accountants' a specific ethnic group, profession or social class and such comments are assumed too often to be fact.

While it is human nature to generalize from personal experience, it can result in rejecting research findings because of having seen a counter-example. The result is raising what ought to be hypothesis to the level of fact. How often has something like the following been said: 'My Uncle Charlie smoked three packs of cigarettes a day and died at 96 riding his bicycle. All this research about cigarettes causing heart disease and lung cancer cannot be true.' Part of the fault for the all too common occurrence of such thinking may be rooted in how researchers present their results to the public as direct cause and effect. Or is it a human trait to believe 'it couldn't happen to me'? Here are some interesting hypotheses for someone looking for a research project.

Many seemingly divergent areas of research employ hypotheses as a point for initiating a study. For example, Cohen and Manion (1989) note that the formulation of a hypothesis or set of questions and then testing it is one approach used in historical research. The main difference is in the use of historical data rather than contemporarily collected data, over which the researcher has more control. Studies related to the past still depend upon the rigorous testing of ideas and sometimes suffer from too many data rather than too few. In such situations, the statement of a hypothesis can assist in focusing a study in a sea of data, helping to take it beyond an exercise in simply collecting facts.

Much later in their book, Cohen and Manion (1989) also note the role of generating questions and hypotheses as one 'method' that can be applied in ethnogenic studies which involve recording and analysing accounts of events and social episodes. The statement of hypotheses can clarify and document the expectations of researchers as they enter a situation, providing a baseline for later conclusions. The use of hypotheses should not be considered as only for quantitative studies; they have useful roles in many approaches.

Stating a hypothesis

Kerlinger (1986) suggests two criteria for acceptable hypotheses, much the same as for questions:

(a)   hypotheses should be statements of possible relationships between variables, and
(b)   these statements should be testable.

The variables must be potentially measurable, and considering the thinking that goes on during the planning of a research project, the variables are likely to have been operationally defined as part of devising a statement of the hypothesis.

In social science research, hypotheses can be placed into one of three general categories:

1   Those that can be confirmed or refuted by direct observation, assuming that the skill to make the appropriate observations exists. For example, we are being watched by extra-terrestrials; video games are harmful to some children (note the 'some').
2   Those that are confirmed or refuted by considering all possible negative alternatives. For example, all Britons are Christians; people enjoy laughing; politicians only lie when their lips move.
3   Those describing a central tendency involving traits of groups. For example, the children in Blogg's School are of average intelligence; workers performing under condition A perform more efficiently than those under condition B. This latter group will require a statement of a null hypothesis (to be discussed below) and inferential statistics to resolve it.

In order to define a hypothesis clearly, it will be necessary at this stage to defined operationally the variables involved. This does not mean that the actual measuring instruments need to be described in detail, but some indication needs to be provided as to how data for the variables will be collected. For example, if the research question consists of a statement relating learner intelligence with some learning outcome, then the hypothesis should be in terms that indicate how intelligence, as well as the learning outcome, is to be measured. The question of validity and reliability of the ultimate instruments used in measurement will be considered in Chapter 4 on data quality.

Whether stated as a question or more formally as a hypothesis, the research problem statement should conform at this level to five important criteria (Open University, 1973). It should be:

1 *Stated clearly*, with definitions of any technical terms and providing the operational definitions of any abstract variables. Ambiguities and vagueness should be avoided.
2 *Testable or resolvable*, since it is a predictor of outcomes of a study or a statement of a question to be answered.
3 *Stated in terms of relationships between variables*, though not necessarily causal relationships. Relationships should be stated clearly, indicating whether it is anticipated that there will be a positive or negative relation.
4 *Limited in scope*, in other words, realistic. The more global the statement of a relationship is, the less likely it will be possible to confirm or refute it. The desire usually exists among researchers that their study will contribute to a broader field of research, but it is unlikely that any single endeavour will solve all the problems.
5 *Not inconsistent with most known facts*, which is best achieved by references to existing literature. Most journal articles are limited by length, so any review of the literature will not necessarily be extensive, though it should provide adequate justification.

One of the problems that a reader will encounter is to decide whether the lack of a stated hypothesis is a matter of technical writing ability or a sin of omission. Sometimes it is possible to infer the hypothesis, while in other cases it will become apparent that there simply was not one.

Cause and effect, or association?

One aspect of scientific investigation is a desire to identify what are the causes of certain human conditions or events, for example, crime, intelligence, divorce, paranoia, rapid learning. Those variables that are suspected of affecting such events or conditions, like heredity, nutrition, good books, are considered *independent variables*. The resulting affected events are the *dependent variables* since they are influenced by (depend on) the other variables and not the other way round. For example, it might be possible that genetics affects intelligence, or even a propensity to crime, but becoming more intelligent or committing crimes will not change one's genetic make-up. Vitamins, or even baked beans, might help children to learn faster in the classroom, but learning faster in the classroom will have no affect on the quality of the vitamins or baked beans. While variables are not often overtly labelled as independent or dependent in reports, the relationship will be implicit.

Are all relationships necessarily causal? No, though sometimes it is

Table 2.1   *Possible relationships between variables*

Research hypothesis	Proposed variables	
	Independent	Dependent
Intelligence is determined primarily by heredity as opposed to environment	Heredity and environment	Intelligence
There is a strong relationship between crime rate and the level of unemployment	Level of unemployment	Crime rate
The preference to go on structured holidays (pre-booked hotels, guided tours, planned events) rather than self-organized ones is related to social class	Social class	Preferences
Encouragement by teacher enhances student performance	Teacher encouragement	Student performance

difficult to tell from the wording just what the author of a report is trying to prove. Relationships can be ones of *association*, where the two variables change together, though there is not a direct cause and effect relationship. For example, it might be hypothesized that tooth decay is affected by increased sunspot activity. In the first place, not everyone would have increased (decreased) tooth decay, so the proposal would be looking for an increase/ decrease in the frequency of tooth decay. It might be possible that the increased radiation resulting from sunspots could directly affect teeth, but then there might be an intermediate stage, such as the radiation affecting calcium uptake in cereal grains that children eat. At this stage, the mechanism is not even suggested and the intent is to determine only whether the relative frequency in the population of tooth decay is at all related to the frequency of sunspots. It would take a different type of research to discover the actual causal mechanism, if the association between the two events were even to exist.

It is not difficult to distinguish a potential independent variable from a dependent one: sunspots might have some direct or indirect affect on tooth decay, but there is no way that the frequency of tooth decay in children could affect the sun. This association, when quantifiable, it often expressed as a *correlation*, a numerical value ranging from +1.00, indicating an exact match between the two events, through zero, indicating no relationship, to −1.00, indicating that as one increases, the other decreases, the size of the number indicating the strength of the association. Therefore, a correlation of 0.82 between two variables would indicate a strong positive association, whereas −0.12 would indicate a weak negative one. Chapter 6 covers this in detail and correlations are mentioned here mainly to emphasize the fact that many relationships are not causal. Thus, the statement of a hypothesis may be in terms of independent and dependent variables, but it may not mean that a potential cause and effect relationship is being investigated (see Table 2.1). Now turn to Activity 2.3.

Activity 2.3

Table 2.1 provides some exemplar studies with the data gathering technique, independent and dependent variables provided. Which describe potential cause and effect relationships and which are possible associations, but not causal? The issue of operationally defining and measuring these variables will be addressed in Chapter 3, so that does not have to be a concern now.

The null hypothesis

There will be situations where the researcher wants to make inferences about a larger population based upon a study carried out on a representative sample of that population. To make such inferences requires the use of statistical tests that compare data about groups of subjects and not individuals. For example, if a researcher wanted to consider mathematical achievement, one approach would be to investigate the performance of a class or group as a whole without focusing on individuals in the class. This requires the use of some indicator of group performance, such as the average (arithmetic mean) of the class performance on an examination: individual scores are not of concern, only the class average.

Consider a hypothesis that suggests a comparison of possible effects (variables) on mathematical achievement. One way to determine whether some variables had a greater effect than others would be to subject two (or more) representative groups to these variables (say different textbooks), and see if there was any difference in achievement of the groups as a whole, as measured through the mathematics examination. The problem for the researcher is that the statistical tests will only tell whether the difference in group examination scores is significant, in other words, whether the difference was large enough to have not occurred by chance. If the significance test says that it is unlikely that the difference could be attributed just to natural variability in scores of two groups having the same characteristics (a significant difference), then it is still up to the researcher to prove that the only possible cause was the distinct learning experiences, here the different textbooks (the variables).

As Campbell and Stanley (1963) note, hypotheses are really never 'confirmed' as the truth, otherwise they would not be hypotheses. Thus a statistical test is really a way of rejecting alternative hypotheses and if the test rejects an undesirable hypothesis (shows no difference), then there is some support for the alternatives, even though these are not absolutely confirmed. In a sense, a hypothesis gains strength by having as many alternative hypotheses as possible proved false, or rejected.

This results in a statement of anticipation of outcome in negative terms: there will be no significant difference, a *null hypothesis*. Thus to reject the null hypothesis means that there is evidence to support the conjecture that there was a difference. Why such a convoluted way of thinking? Statistical tests only give *probabilities* of something occurring, so the statistical test will only resolve whether or not two or more groups probably belong to the same group after different experiences. Thus by saying it is highly probable that they belong to the same group means that there was no significant difference. To reject this null hypothesis means there probably was a difference and they probably no longer belong to the same group (for this trait). This would lend support to the hypothesis of interest, but not confirm that it is absolutely true.

Campbell and Stanley (1963) recognize that not being able to confirm a hypothesis directly goes against a scientist's experience and attitudes. In such complex situations as are found in social science research where there are so many possible hypotheses because there are so many possible variables, there must be degrees of confirmation. 'Well-established' theories simply have few, if any, plausible alternatives left after extensive investigations. Positive reinforcement does encourage human behaviour, but the widespread acceptance of this statement is based upon an extensive body of research, some contending with such problems as what constitutes 'positive' reinforcement for certain groups may not be true for others. For example, one child deprived of attention at home may consider a rap on the knuckles with a ruler as positive reinforcement for his actions: he received attention rather than being ignored by the teacher. On the other hand, another child would be devastated by such violence. Again, careful definition of the variables is necessary. The control of variables in a study is an exercise by the researcher in making alternative hypotheses implausible. The discussion of the null hypothesis will continue in later chapters, as it is recognized that it is a difficult concept to grasp.

One other source of confusion arises from the use of the word 'significant'. Just because a study reports a statistical significance does not necessarily mean that it has found anything of sociological, psychological or educational significance. For example, using large samples, it is possible to have statistically significant correlations that are very small. As a case in point, it has been found in Britain that the correlation between A-level examination results (taken at age 18+ as part of selection for university entrance in the United Kingdom) and subsequent level of success at university as indicated by degree classification, was of the order of 0.20 (Bourner and Hamad, 1987). This was statistically significant, even though numerically small, primarily because of the very large sample. While the null hypothesis would be rejected (this correlation occurred by chance alone), a correlation of this size means very little in practical terms, except to other researchers looking for ideas for more research. The actual educational significance lies in that there is such a *small* relationship between A-level results and subsequent class of university degree achieved. It is not a good predictor.

There is no necessity for all hypotheses to be stated as null hypotheses, but if the intent is to make inferences to a larger population through a study that collects data to be processed statistically, then a null hypothesis is in order. While a general hypothesis may propose a cause and effect relationship, a null hypothesis should not, since all that the resulting statistical tests will be able to determine will be whether or not the relationship occurred by chance or not. The strength of the proof for the causal hypothesis will depend more on how well the researcher controlled or eliminated all the other possible causes. Now try your hand at Activity 2.4.

Activity 2.4

Below are three statements of research hypotheses; read each in turn, considering its merits, then pass judgement on its quality *before* reading the model answers at the end of the chapter. Since these statements are taken out of context, you may disagree with the evaluation supplied, which is quite reasonable assuming you can defend yours.

(a)   Group study contributes to a higher level of achievement in a class than independent study.
(b)   The amount of practice required to master a skill will have no effect on motivation to learn.
(c)   Middle-class children more often than lower-class children will avoid finger painting tasks.

What is fact and what is hypothesis?

Unless one is well informed and reads or listens critically, it is often difficult to determine what is fact and what is conjecture or hypothesis, particularly in public statements that tend to be unsubstantiated and taken out of context. For example, in the popular press, Beauchamp (1988) presented an interesting example to consider,

> A report on the effects of the new Housing Bill on homeless people by the West London Homeless Group says: '. . . It adds weight to the view that ministers do not recognise homelessness as being a problem and that the problem is a product of feckless councils and feckless individuals.'

Such statements require careful dissection. The use of English makes this sound as if there is a contradiction in that the 'problem' is not recognized, but its cause is. In reality, it appears that the word 'problem' is used in two ways, the first time it refers to homelessness as a condition that might or might not be treated directly, and the second time 'problem' refers to a possible cause of homelessness. Let us consider the statement as it was probably intended. If ministers (politicians, not clergymen) do think that the 'problem' is fecklessness as described, do *they* take it to be fact or hypothesis? But even before this, the question can be asked, is it a fact that ministers do not see that homelessness is a directly treatable problem, or is this really a statement of hypothesis? With no supporting evidence either way, it seems that the best one can do is to treat both these statements – the assumption that ministers have a lack of recognition of homelessness as a directly treatable condition *and* what they identify as a treatable problem (the cause of homelessness) is fecklessness – as possible conflicting hypotheses.

While the general public accepts or ignores such statements (a hypothesis supported by the fact that such statements continually appear), possibly because there is a general feeling that political statements are not expected to be substantiated (another hypothesis), research papers generally do not put forward unsubstantiated statements as fact. More appropriately, hypotheses are presented as starting points for research. Having said this, the reader of research can gain a certain amount of skill in distinguishing fact from hypothesis by simply reading the popular press as suggested in Activity 2.5.

Activity 2.5

Select a current newspaper article describing someone's stand on an issue, that of a politician or one expressed in an editorial. Read it analytically, particularly considering supposed statements of fact, noting which of these are truly factual statements and which are really untested conjecture or hypotheses.

Criteria for evaluating research questions and hypotheses

Below are the five criteria levels selected to delineate levels of quality of the statement of research questions and/or hypotheses that will be used when evaluating research articles:

Valid question or hypothesis based on accepted theory with well-justified and referenced support. The validity of the statement will have to be judged based upon your knowledge of the field and the literature, but this is still the strongest basis for a hypothesis. This also assumes that the statement conforms to the five criteria outlined earlier, that hypotheses and questions are stated clearly, testable or resolvable, stated in terms of relationships between variables, limited in scope, and not inconsistent with most known facts.

Valid question or hypothesis based on own theory, well justified. The validity will have to be based primarily upon your knowledge of the discipline and your judgement as to the soundness of the rationale or justification. A new theory may be extrapolating into new areas or contradicting established ones, thus there should be a strong argument for it.

Credible question/hypothesis but alternatives possible, or too extensive/ global, or support missing. This level covers three 'sins': (a) there are more valid alternative hypotheses that you can identify; (b) the statement is so global for it to be unlikely that a single study could resolve the issue; or (c) there is a hypothesis or research question stated that on the surface seems reasonable, but there is no justification.

Weak question/hypothesis, or poorly stated, or justified with inappropriate references. (a) The question or hypothesis is questionable from the view of it being inconsistent with previous research, or unreasonable in terms of your knowledge of the discipline; (b) it is poorly stated in abstract terms, with variables not clearly or not operationally defined; or (c) the researcher has references that do not really provide credible support.

No question or hypothesis stated, or inconsistent with known facts. Occasionally, one will find a report that has no research question or hypothesis stated. As noted above, either the writer has failed to state the intent of the study or was just 'data dredging'. In other words, data were collected with no hypothesis or research question in mind and the author is trying to find some relationship. Even so, there should be a statement or question to this effect. The last section of this chapter elaborates on this omission.

Occasionally (rarely in refereed journals) one will find a paper purporting to investigate relationships that contradict established research. There is the chance that something new has been found, but rarely do we ever encounter 'earth-shattering discoveries' in the social sciences. These can occur when someone's beliefs are very strong, such as in articles that purportedly prove the general inferiority of certain ethnic or racial groups. Sources publishing articles of this quality may not be refereed or may have a strong bias.

Dredging for variables

Rigorous experimentalists will state that all studies need hypotheses. Other researchers will maintain that there are times when less well-defined studies are necessary to allow one to look for possible relationships and hypotheses. Studies of the second type still have demands made of them in terms of rules to follow. Slevin and Stuart (1978) describe three types of study that involve data dredging, where questions or hypotheses may be missing:

1 *Snooping* – testing all the (perhaps infinite) predesignated hypotheses possible in a set of data. There are specific rigorous statistical tests for this, so there is at least no reason for not identifying the hypotheses.

2 *Fishing* – an approach of the survey analyst used to choose which of a number of potential variables to use in an explanation. Computer programs, for example for correlation and regression, make such a task easier. The objection is that by selecting to report just some of the variables, the research may produce misleading results, suggesting probabilities that are much higher than justified by the test. This will be considered in greater detail in Chapter 6. On the positive side, the process can be a starting point for future more experimentally based research by identifying potential variables. Let it suffice to say that if this is the intent, then the researcher still has questions to ask and should admit to fishing.

3 *Hunting* – this approach has no predesignated set of variables to investigate, and subsequently, there are no *appropriate* statistical tests. It can involve searching data, for example demographic data not collected by the researcher, for some relationship(s) worth testing, or testing one hypothesis in several sets of data until something is found. This is one argument for replicating studies, as it is not always possible to tell when someone has been hunting, carrying out a series of studies and discarding data that produces no significance. While this process may also be of use to the survey analyst in helping to identify potential variables, it is the reluctance to admit it and make unwarranted claims for one's results that is the sin. A question can still be stated and the process of hunting admitted.

Summary

This chapter has introduced the criteria for judging the adequacy and quality of research questions and hypotheses, as described in articles and reports. One of your problems as a reader and evaluator when encountering the lack of either or both of these, is whether there were any to begin with, or whether there was an omission in writing the report. Without a clear statement of the research question(s) and hypotheses, it will be difficult to evaluate the logical consistency of operational definitions and the quality of the data subsequently collected. Clear questions and hypotheses provide a sound base line for you when reading a report, but sometimes these must be isolated from the text by the reader: it may be that the questions are implied and not marked with a nice clear question mark. Activity 2.6 gives you have an opportunity to apply these criteria to a report or article.

Activity 2.6

Choose up to three articles from your own literature search and rate them according to the quality of statement of research question or hypothesis, using a photocopy of the first column of the Profiling Sheet (at the end of this chapter). Mark your choice of level by circling it. You should justify your rating in each case and include comments where appropriate. Compare your ratings and rationales with colleagues.

References

Adams, D. (1979) *The Hitch Hiker's Guide to the Galaxy*. Pan Books.

Beauchamp, M. (1988) 'Hard facts to sleep on', *Guardian*, 25 May, p. 21.

Blum, M.L. and Foos, P.W. (1986) *Data Gathering: Experimental Methods Plus*. Harper & Row.

Bourner, T. and Hamad, M. (1987) *Entry Qualifications and Degree Performance*. London, CNAA.

Campbell, D.T. and Stanley, J.C. (1963) *Experimental and Quasi-experimental Designs in Educational Research*. Rand McNally.

Cohen, L. and Manion, L. (1989) Research Methods in Education, 3rd edn. Routledge.

Greer, S. (1978) 'On the selection of problems'. in J. Bynner and K.M. Stribley (eds), *Social Research: Principles and Procedures*. Longman. pp. 48–52.

Kerlinger, F.N. (1986) *Foundations of Behavioral Research*, 3rd edn. Holt, Rinehart & Winston.

Open University (1973) *Methods of Educational Enquiry, E341. Block 2: Research Design*. Open University Press. pp. 19–21.

Popper, K.R. (1978) 'The unity of method', in J. Bynner and K.M. Stribley (eds), *Social Research: Principles and Procedures*. Longman. pp. 17–24.

Slevin, C. and Stuart, A. (1978) 'Data-dredging procedures in survey analysis', in J. Bynner and K.M. Stribley (eds), *Social Research: Principles and Procedures*. Longman. pp. 278–84.

Activity model answers

Activity 2.2

(a) This is a poor question since it is not going to be possible to test this empirically. First, 'democratic education' will be difficult to define in operational (observable) terms and, secondly, where is one going to find a non-democratic education against which to compare?

(b) This one is reasonable since it states a possible relationship, the variables are unambiguous, and it is testable.

(c) The term 'best' is ambiguous and would be improved even by referring to 'better than' something else, assuming the something else was definable and the resulting relationship could be empirically tested.

Activity 2.4

(a) The variables 'how they learn' and 'how much they learn' are unambiguous and potentially definable, and the hypothesis is testable. Whether it becomes a case study (two convenient groups in the researcher's own school) or broader enquiry using a number of representative groups is irrelevant at this point, as will be seen in Chapter 3.

(b) This is a statement in the null hypothesis form, implying that the two variables, amount of practice required and motivation, are not related. Assuming that a test of motivation to learn can be devised, then this is a reasonable and testable hypothesis.

(c) Kerlinger (1986) suggests that this hypothesis is one level away from the actual hypothesis; he says 'finger painting behaviour is in part a function of social class'. Thus the above is a prediction based upon a broader hypothesis.

Profiling Sheet: Evaluating Questions and Hypotheses (to photocopy) © Thomas R. Black 1993

Article: _____

Question/hypothesis
(*Actions 1–3*)

Valid question or
hypothesis based on
accepted theory
with well-justified
and referenced
support

Valid question or
hypothesis based on
own theory, well
justified

Credible question/
hypothesis but
alternatives
possible, or too
extensive/global, or
support missing

Weak question/
hypothesis, or
poorly stated, or
justified with
inappropriate
references

No question or
hypothesis stated,
or inconsistent with
known facts

Comments:

3
Representativeness: How Far Can You Generalize?

After determining what the purpose of the research is, the reader of a report must answer another question: to whom are the results intended to apply? To what group will the conclusions be justifiably relevant? The answer to this may be partly determined by the initial research questions asked: were there a few variables to be investigated or many? Often the limitations of resources (money, time and effort available) determine whom the subjects are and subsequently how far the results can be generalized. Looking ahead, the ultimate level of generalization decided upon will have had an influence on what research tools and types of analysis were chosen by the researcher. This chapter will consider both the implications of how the subjects for a study were chosen and the criteria for rating articles and reports on this aspect. Later chapters will consider the consequence of the choices made at this stage.

Populations and samples

As human beings, we tend to go through life drawing conclusions from our experiences. We try a tandoori chicken dish, we meet a couple of Germans, we drive a Rover car, but it is not possible to taste every tandoori chicken, meet every German, nor drive every Rover car. So generalizations tend to be made on the basis of these limited samples and it is decided that tandoori is delightful, Germans do not speak much English, and Rover cars steer differently from other cars. The only problem is, were our samples truly typical? Are our conclusions warranted, and extended fairly and appropriately to all tandooris, all Germans, and all Rover cars? What happens when we eat at a different tandoori restaurant, meet yet another German, and drive a Rover made in a different year? When our samples are taken in such a haphazard way, it is unlikely that our conclusions or inferences based upon a single or limited number of encounters are necessarily going to be valid for all tandoori chickens, for Germans in general or for all Rover cars. In order to find a solution to this dilemma, let us first consider some common words that have specific technical meanings in research, terminology that should help the reader understand the problems associated with drawing valid conclusions.

The larger groups to which generalizations are extended are called *populations* and, for research purposes, they must be defined by the author of any report or article. Common everyday use of the term population tends to mean that people are grouped or classified by national, racial or ethnic origins. But a research population could consist of all 13-year-old children in Scotland, all males between 21 and 31 in the United States, all 1987 Rover cars. It is up to the researcher to identify and describe adequately the population to which the results are intended to apply and, like all other aspects of research, any such claim must be justified. Secondly, the term *sample* tends to imply a group selected from a larger population in some way so as to ensure that, for the characteristic(s) being investigated, the group is typical. This turns out not to be a trivial task.

Characteristics of populations and samples

Without deviating too far, a brief mention of a parallel consideration should be made. It is not too difficult to define the characteristics of a population so that it could be decided whether or not an individual actually belongs or not. It is possible to define rigorously what constitutes a tandoori chicken dish (by its ingredients), a German (by his/her passport) and a Rover car (by the badge on the front). We can argue about special cases but, ultimately, the decision is binary: the individual belongs or does not belong.

The real problem arises when one begins to look at characteristics of these groups: saying a tandoori is 'good' or 'bad', a German can or cannot speak English, or a Rover car steers or does not steer (assuming it is road worthy) does not mean much. It is harder to classify them in such a binary way because the categories are too difficult to define. This is where some sort of measurement of variables emerges. For example, it is more realistic to find an average rating (say on a scale of 1 to 10) of tandoori chicken dishes in a restaurant, an average English language proficiency examination score, and an average rating of quality of steering on Rover cars. The 'average' is a measure of *central tendency*; in other words, it is an indication of what the group does as a whole. No two meals, no two Germans and no two Rover cars are exactly the same (though the differences in some cases may be hard to detect). So if we want to talk about the group as a whole, then the average is often used: the group 'tends' to have a certain characteristic. There are several different 'averages' or measures of central tendency that we can use, but this is a topic for a later chapter.

When such numerical characteristics are assigned to populations, for example, the average IQ test score for the whole population, then they are called *parameters*. On the other hand, if the characteristics apply to a sample, continuing the example, the average of a selected representative group, then they are referred to as *statistics* (Chase, 1985; Open University, 1973). Since most data are collected on samples from populations, and inferences are sometimes made about the population from these samples, we hear the term statistics used quite frequently when referring to data presented in articles and reports.

Selecting samples

How a researcher actually chooses a sample from a population will determine whether the members of the sample group can be considered to be truly *representative* of that population. In other words, the average (measure of central tendency) found for the sample should be very close to the population average, if the sample is truly representative. Thus, if a representative sample (say 50) of all Germans was acquired, it would be expected that their average score on an English language proficiency examination would be very close to what we would find for the whole population (all Germans) if such data could be collected. Often population parameters with which to compare are not available and the researcher must depend upon the rigour of the sampling process to justify the representativeness of the sample. Therefore, from data collected on a highly representative sample of Danes, a researcher should be able to calculate a good estimate of the average annual income in Denmark. There are a few exceptions, such as IQ tests which tend to be designed to provide a population average score of 100.

Sample representativeness can be achieved through one of a number of processes of selection that are designed to ensure this characteristic, most of which are based upon some aspect of random selection. Kerlinger's (1986) definition provides a starting point, '*Random sampling* is that method of drawing a portion (sample) of a population . . . so that each member of the population . . . has an equal chance of being selected.'

This is incredibly difficult if not impossible to achieve for most human populations that we would wish to define for an investigation. For example, if a study were to consist of collecting data on a specific group of easily available 13-year-olds, like Mary Blogg's secondary school physics class in Birmingham, then the results would pertain to the entire population: that specific group of available 13-year-olds in her physics class in Birmingham. The group cannot be considered to be a sample that is representative of any larger population. To extend research conclusions from a study on a sample and make inferences about a larger population requires that the sample is shown to be representative of that population, in other words, typical in all relevant characteristics, variables or aspects. This presents researchers with practical problems. Using the example of 13-year-old secondary school students, where would we even get a complete list of all 13-year-olds from which to select? It does not exist, any more than many such lists, or it changes from day to day (Blum and Foos, 1986). Consequently, the above definition is not very functional.

Kerlinger (1986) does provide a more realistic definition, '*Random sampling* is that method of drawing a portion (sample) of a population so that all possible samples of fixed size *n* have the same probability of being selected.' As we will see, this more general definition allows some flexibility in the actual methods to be considered below. For our study of 13-year-olds, it means that randomly selecting *groups* (classes) of 13-year-olds from all possible groups (classes) would provide what can be considered to be a representative sample.

Unfortunately, this stipulation of equal probability raises a problem, which at first tends to make one uneasy about the whole business of sampling. Basically, even when taking a random sample, there is a finite probability that the resulting group will *not* be representative. This is one of the arguments for replicating a study: the more random samples taken, the less likely it will be to get non-representative samples and the stronger the justification for the results. As Kerlinger (1986) notes, while there is no guarantee that the random sample is representative, there is a much higher likelihood that random selection will provide a representative sample than one that is purposively selected. Thus, a researcher is in a much stronger position when using a process of selection that consists of some form of randomization to consider the sample representative, than one who does not. As the various types of selection commonly employed by researchers are considered below, the advantages, pitfalls and implications for relative representativeness of each will be considered.

Randomization

Having frequently used the term 'random' and extolled the virtues of having randomness, it is now time to describe some processes for actually acquiring a representative sample. Part of the problem lies in what is meant by 'randomness'. Kerlinger (1986) provides the following definition: '*randomness* means that there is no known law, capable of being expressed in language, that correctly describes or explains events and their outcomes.' Since randomness is a concept that forms the basis of much of inferential statistics, this is one definition you may want to refer to again. When selecting a sample, randomness is often achieved through schemes based on tables of random numbers, lists of non-repeating numbers which are often created by computer programs that are mathematically based. The simplest approach would be to use a random numbers table, such as Table 3.1, and begin at the beginning. While the list itself is a list of numbers at random, if you started at the beginning each time you used it, you would end up with the same sequence of numbers each time. A researcher doing this would be open to criticism since the lists would be predictable, and would not be considered random. So a little more randomness must be inserted into the process. Typically, if a list of 20 random numbers were needed in order to choose a representative sample of 20 students from a class of 100, a researcher could close his/her eyes,

Table 3.1　A short three-digit random numbers table of numbers between 0 and 999

777	841	707	655	297	947	945	743	697	633
297	522	872	029	710	687	614	660	555	489
672	573	065	306	207	112	703	768	377	178
465	436	070	187	267	566	640	669	291	071
914	487	548	262	860	675	846	300	171	191
820	042	451	108	905	340	437	347	999	997
731	819	473	811	795	591	393	769	678	858
937	434	506	749	268	237	997	343	587	922
248	627	730	055	348	711	204	425	046	655
762	805	801	329	005	671	799	372	427	699

poke a finger at the table of three-digit numbers (thus randomly choosing where to start) and then take the next 20 numbers.

Using Table 3.1, this would be difficult since it uses three-digit numbers, so alternatively, the list could be treated as a continuous string of two-digit numbers. Then the first two digits of the number chosen could be used to determine how far down an even longer list, of say 300, to jump to select the first person. For example, if the last number of the second column were picked, 805, it begins with 80. Starting at the top of the list of 300, number 80 would join the sample. Using the 5 from 805 and the 7 from the first digit of the next number on the list, 707, jump 57 down the list to number 137. Then jump another 07 to number 144, and so on until 20 students have been selected. Obviously, it is possible to reach the end of the list before getting 20 names. Solution: just continue counting from the beginning again as if it were one continuous list. The proof of randomness is, if you start somewhere else in the table, you will get a different group of 20 students. The fact that one group may overlap with another, and some students could appear in two randomly selected groups, does not diminish the randomness, it is the fact that the *groups* are different. How the numbers in a random numbers table are used to select groups is only limited by imagination: one can go across the table instead of down, or even go up. The test of the validity of any random number generation scheme is whether or not you end up with two identical groups by starting at two different places in the table: you should not! Other schemes are described in standard texts on statistics and research design. Do Activity 3.1 before moving on to the discussion of different sampling methods that employ randomness.

Random samples: several types

There are various ways to apply randomization (which is sometimes referred to as probability sampling) that can be employed to achieve a sample that can be considered representative (Blum and Foos, 1986; Cohen and Manion, 1989; Kerlinger, 1986). Some of these will deviate

---

Activity 3.1

This will give you an opportunity to prove to yourself that 'randomization' can produce a unique sequence of numbers that could be used to select subjects for a study:

(a)   Use Table 3.1 to produce three lists of random two-digit numbers. Are the lists different? Is there any overlap?

(b)   If you have a pocket calculator that will produce random numbers, produce three similar lists, and answer the same questions.

---

from selecting directly from a given population, avoiding the problems of beginning with enormously large lists that may not even exist:

1   *Simple random sampling* does involve taking a random sample directly from the population, achieving Kerlinger's first definition stated earlier of each member of a population having an equal chance of being selected. This approach is limited by the availability of a complete list of the population, one that could be very large and not feasible or even possible to obtain.

2   *Stratified random sampling* consists of taking random samples from various strata in society, such as men and women, employed and unemployed etc. This depends on what the researcher is interested in: does the colour of a Rover affect its steering? Does the age, social and educational background or hair colour of Germans potentially relate to their ability to speak English? Some strata are obviously more relevant than others and thus possible relations are worth investigating. This is actually the result of defining different sub-populations within a larger population.

3   *Cluster sampling* takes into account the difficulty of sampling from a large population (say, all secondary pupils) by randomly selecting clusters of subjects. For example, it would be possible to randomly select 20 schools nationwide and then include all the pupils in these schools for a study.

4   *Stage sampling* is an extension of cluster sampling and is often used in selecting subjects for a survey. This involves successive random selections; for example, a researcher might randomly select ten local education authorities or school districts, randomly select three schools in each, and randomly select ten teachers in each school, giving a total of 300 teachers.

Combinations of the last three processes might even be applied: for example, ten local education authorities or school districts could be randomly selected, then in each of them, three boys, girls and mixed schools would be randomly selected (assuming that there were equal

numbers of each in the areas chosen), and finally five teachers in each
school randomly chosen, giving 450 teachers, 150 from each type of school.
Now try your hand at Activity 3.2.

Activity 3.2

Identify the population and classify each of the following descriptions
of samples as one or a combination of:

(a)   random sampling from whole population,
(b)   stratified random sampling,
(c)   cluster sampling,
(d)   stage sampling.

1   A random selection of 120 male and female social workers
    selected from the union roles.
2   The young people in 16 randomly selected youth groups.
3   A random selection of 100 teachers in a local education authority.
4   Random samples of 20 unemployed men and women between the
    ages of 18 and 26.
5   Six groups of 30 14-year-old pupils, each group's members
    randomly selected from one of six randomly selected schools from
    a list of all boys, girls and mixed schools in England.

Sample size

Having unambiguously defined a population, a research report should
describe the size of the sample. Are there any criteria for determining just
how large a sample should be? As Kerlinger (1986) notes, when an average
or other statistic is calculated for a sample, the researcher is estimating the
value (parameter) for the whole population. Thus, there will be some
error, which will be dependent upon the size of the sample, as shown in
Figure 3.1. The smaller the sample, the greater the error and vice versa.
For example, if you wanted an estimate of average height of all 13-year-
olds in a school, you would expect a much more accurate estimation from a
random sample of 30 than from a random sample of five. Thus the larger
the sample, the more precise the statistic will be – in other words, closer to
the population parameter. Chapters 6 and 7 will show just how the sample
size affects statistical tests but, in general, it is to the researcher's benefit to
have as large a sample as resources will allow.

Non-random samples

There are several techniques which provide less justifiably representative
samples, though some of these are better than others. Sometimes these are

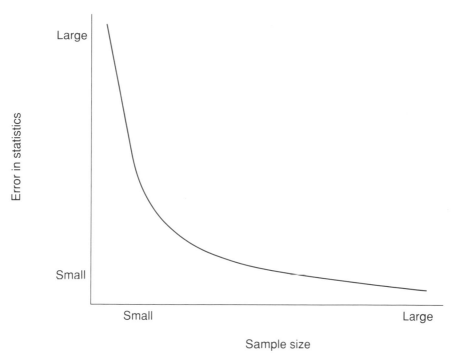

Figure 3.1 *Rough relationship between sample size and error, where error is considered to be the deviation of sample values (statistics) from population values (parameters) (after Kerlinger, 1986).*

used because the cost of taking a random sample is too great, or it is very difficult to obtain a complete list of the members of the whole population. The ones described below are typical of techniques that have been applied in research articles and reports (Cohen and Manion, 1989; Kerlinger, 1986), some providing more representative samples than others:

Purposive sampling The researcher hand-picks subjects on the basis of traits to give what is felt or believed to be a representative sample. To achieve this would require all the relevant variables or traits to be identified so the sample would include a cross-section of persons possessing these. For example, a sample of teachers in a local education authority could be acquired by individually selecting from a database a set of 30 teachers in local schools with the intent to include a variety of ages, subjects taught and years of experience. The advantage is that one can possibly better ensure a cross-section of the population in a small sample, which might otherwise miss certain categories of persons. The main limitations to this approach are that a researcher may not have identified all contributing variables and characteristics, or individual bias may prevail when carrying out the selection.

Quota sampling The researcher non-randomly selects subjects from identified strata until desired numbers are reached. For example, a survey might include interviewing the first 20 people who, in each situation, answer their door in: a housing estate, a set of high-rise apartments, a set of semi-detached (duplex) houses etc. An extension of this would involve taking into account more than one variable, like 10 men and 10 women as well as type of house, which is referred to as *dimensional sampling*. Such an approach ensures that each group is of the same size, which can be important for some inferential statistical tests. The disadvantage is that the numbers may not reflect the true proportions of sub-populations in the whole population.

Convenience, accidental or volunteer sampling The researcher takes a group or individuals that are available, like the local PTA, three classes in a local school or any students willing to come in after class (a seemingly common practice amongst psychologists who use their own university student volunteers). Radio and television programmes have used the technique of inviting the audience to telephone one of several available numbers as a means of registering a view, while newspapers have invited readers to respond to questions. Moore (1991) describes one such programme presented by Ann Landers, the advice columnist in the United States, who invited readers to respond to the question 'If you had to do it over again, would you have children?' With 10,000 respondents and 70 per cent saying 'No!', parenthood seemed in danger. Yet a random sample of 1,373 parents by *Newsday* magazine found that 91 per cent would have children again. The question arises, is the volume response more representative than the randomly selected one? It is often difficult to convince the public that vociferous minorities are not representative. Basically, the 'researchers', if they could be called that, are not dealing with a sample, but a small population, and do not really have the grounds on which to make inferences to a larger population. It is very difficult, if not impossible, to justify that such a group is truly representative of a larger population, no matter what its size. As the advertisement says, 'Can one million people be wrong?' Maybe not, but then there is no guarantee that they are representative of the whole country either.

Snowball sampling The researcher identifies a small number of subjects with the required characteristics, who in turn identify others etc. This is of value when a researcher has little idea of the size or extent of a population, or there simply may be no records of population size; for example, such groups as illegal drug users, illegal immigrants or homosexual teachers. The disadvantage of depending upon such a sample is that the researcher will have difficulty in defending the representativeness of the sample.

Some samples of populations for you to consider are given in Activity 3.3.

Activity 3.3

Identify the intended population and classify each of the numbered descriptions of samples as *one or more* of the following:

(a) random sampling, possibly from whole population,
(b) stratified random sampling,
(c) cluster sampling,
(d) stage sampling,
(e) purposive sampling,
(f) quota sampling,
(g) convenience, accidental or volunteer sampling,
(h) snowball sampling.

1 A study on stress among social workers started with the random selection of 120 male and female social workers selected from the county's employee register. Ultimately, 95 per cent of the men and 85 per cent of the women responded to the questionnaire.

2 The young people in 16 randomly selected youth groups. Actual interviews were conducted by setting up a network of young persons, starting with a few who subsequently talked their friends into participating.

3 A random selection of 50 High Streets in villages across Britain (or Main Streets in small towns across America) were chosen and researchers sent to each to interview 50 shoppers all on the same Saturday morning, obtaining responses to 20 questions from a pre-planned questionnaire sheet.

4 Sets of 30 pupils randomly selected from two each of chosen boys, girls, and mixed schools, recommended as typical of county schools by the Inspectorate.

The sample: is it representative?

Many public surveying organizations use the telephone as a tool for contacting their sample, be it for predicting election results or market research for a new product. Two sources of numbers exist: (a) a random selection from the telephone directory, which will not have all the numbers since some people have unlisted ones, and (b) computer-generated dialling using a random number, but not everyone has a telephone. In both situations, it is worthwhile remembering the earlier definition of random sampling, and then asking what are the populations for each of these samples? For (a), those with telephone numbers listed in a directory; for (b) those who have telephones. Moore (1991) points out a number of sources of error using the second technique. First, in America, 7 per cent of households do not have telephones. Secondly, when no one answers, the system moves on to a new number, thus reaching those who are easiest to reach. The result of this in one political survey was that 37 per cent of those who answered were men, when the population is roughly half and half. Women tended to answer the household telephone much more frequently than men. Such errors are referred to by Moore as *sampling errors*, since they are the result of actually taking the sample, resulting in a non-random sample.

Alternatively, potentially misleading data can be collected, the cause of the errors being unrelated to the method of sampling. The sample may be random and representative, but the resulting data may not be complete or accurate. Moore (1991) calls these *non-sampling errors* and provides four categories of sources:

1 *Missing data* may be due to the inability to contact a selected subject or not all the selected subjects choosing to participate, resulting in volunteers.
2 *Response errors* will arise from subjects providing inaccurate information, for example about their age or income. Alternatively, the questions may be misunderstood, a problem addressed in Chapter 4 on data quality.
3 *Processing errors* can arise from coding data or entering it into computer files.
4 *Method of data collection*, includes such problems as timing of a survey, wording of questions and what medium will be used (postal survey, telephone or personal interview). These are all related to data quality and will be discussed in Chapter 4.

With eight types of sampling described, and some of the pitfalls identified, what does one expect to find when reading research papers and journal articles? Often, a specific sampling strategy is planned, but when all the data have been collected, the actual sample may be something of a combination of the above. For example, a study was planned to investigate the effects of a new curriculum project on learning among 13-year-olds. Cluster sampling was used to choose randomly 12 classes of children in the county. Random assignment was employed so that half the classes would use the new curriculum materials and half would use existing materials. The children's achievement of stated objectives was tested both before and after using the materials. When all the results were collected, it was found that 80 per cent of the children had used assigned materials and taken both tests. What type of sample did this study really have? It started as representative and ended with volunteers, though the relative representativeness could still be maintained if the researcher were to determine and report on why 20 per cent did not participate. If the reason were totally unrelated to the study, like a flu epidemic, then the results could legitimately be extended to the whole population. But if it were found that the 20 per cent were mostly in one half of the study and the children did not participate because of lack of teacher cooperation, then the researcher needs to answer the question 'why?'. If the reason for non-cooperation related to some aspect of teachers' attitudes towards the project, for example they did not like the materials or the tests were felt to interfere with class work, then it becomes more difficult to defend the representativeness of the remaining part of the sample.

Random assignment: one means of controlling variables

Randomization has another role in research, one that actually follows selecting the sample(s). For truly experimental designs, there will be situations where it is necessary to divide a sample into equivalent sub-groups so that one or more can receive a 'treatment', to use a medical term, and the remaining constitute the control, not receiving any treatment, or a placebo. The random assignment of subjects to sub-groups prevents any bias and maintains the representativeness of each of the subsequent sub-groups. The resulting tests after the treatment will determine whether all the groups *still* belong to the same population (presumably the treatments had no effect) or that they no longer belong to the same population. In the latter case, the researcher must prove that the treatment(s) were the only possible cause of this difference.

Random assignment is one technique for endeavouring to prevent *confounding*, allowing uncontrolled factors to influence the outcome or validity of the conclusions of a study. Confounding can be caused by *extraneous variables*, which are unanticipated independent variables(s) of no interest to the study that influence the results. Table 3.2 provides some examples of studies and potential confounding factors. The reader of a report should always be aware of the possibility of extraneous variables. When suspected, it is often difficult to tell whether the researchers failed to identify them early enough to control them, or that it was not possible, for one reason or another, to control them even though they were identified. Kerlinger (1986) suggests three ways of controlling extraneous variables:

(a) choose subjects that are as homogeneous as possible for the independent variable(s);
(b) randomly assign subjects to groups or conditions, or randomly assign conditions to groups, for experimental designs;
(c) match subjects for potential extraneous variables when assigning them to groups, so all groups have an equal influence, for example equal percentages of high, medium and low IQ subjects.

Confounding and extraneous variables will be addressed in more detail in Chapter 8 on drawing conclusions. At this point, as a reader, it is simply worthwhile to note that randomization can be applied not only at the original selection of the sample, but also to the creation of representative sub-groups to prevent confounding by extraneous variables. Please see Activity 3.4 (p. 54).

Table 3.2   *Examples of studies with potential independent, dependent and confounding variables identified (extended from Table 2.1)*

Research hypothesis	Potential variables		Possible confounding factors
	Independent	Dependent	
Intelligence is determined primarily by heredity as opposed to environment	Heredity and environment	Intelligence	Inability to manipulate the environments of any groups
There is a strong relationship between crime rate and the level of unemployment	Level of unemployment	Crime rate	Unpredicted events: racial unrest and riots
The preference to go on structured holidays (pre-booked hotels, guided tours, planned events) rather than self-organized ones is related to social class	Social class	Preferences	Non-respondents to the survey through the holiday booking firms
Encouragement by teacher enhances student performance	Teacher encouragement	Student performance	Not all teachers taught the same age group

Activity 3.4

Consider the potential confounding factors in Table 3.2: which are extraneous variables potentially subject to control, sampling or non-sampling errors, or a combination? It is possible to acquire extraneous variables because of sampling or non-sampling errors.

The consequences of sampling: a link with hypotheses

As noted earlier, the aim of sampling is to ensure that the acquired statistics will be as close as possible to the population parameters. While it is possible that a given sample will provide statistics that are *exactly* the same as the population parameters, it is not likely. At the same time, the statistics should be very close to parameter values. In fact, as will be seen in Chapter 6, it is possible to quantify how close. If one knows what the population parameters are (for example, IQ tests are designed to have a population average score of 100), there are tests that will tell you whether or not a sample is probably representative of the population. Note the term probably. The unnerving aspect of statistics is that nothing is exact and it is necessary continually to think in terms of 'probably'.

Using the example of IQ test scores, if a sample of 20 15-year-old students was selected and a researcher wanted to know whether or not the group (not individuals) was typical with respect to IQ of all students aged 15, the question would be answered in terms of probability. The null hypothesis could be stated something like 'There is no significant difference between the average score for this sample and the population average score for IQ.' The statistical test will tell what the probability is that the group is part of the population. If the probability turns out to be 5 per cent or less, then the difference between the sample and the population is considered significant, the group is probably *not* part of the population for this trait, and therefore not a representative group. As noted earlier, it is often not possible to carry out this test simply because population parameters are usually not available, but it is a useful one when a researcher does have them. Some reports may actually use such a test to justify the representativeness of a sample. The actual test, a mathematically simple one, will be covered in Chapter 6.

Why generalize?

The value of being able to generalize results has been questioned, in particular with reference to evaluation studies that tend to be fraught with local variables (Guba, 1978). On the other hand, the situation can exist where there is such tight control on all the variables to ensure generalizability that any parallel group would be rare. Also, Guba (1978) maintains that in extreme situations, things change so radically that not only is generalizability difficult, but that replication is impossible. But whether this is true is really up to the consumer of the report to determine.

Not everyone would agree with the suggestion that generalizability is of declining value to researchers. Some of the purposes of research include building models, identifying variables and their interrelations, and generally trying to enhance understanding of human behaviour. The more generalizable the results, the greater the possibility that one can begin to resolve conflicting hypotheses. Without generalizability of results, social science research in general will tend to limp along, not benefiting from the efforts of others, collecting results on a piecemeal basis. It is not easy to design a study so that the results will apply to larger groups, and this chapter has introduced only some of the approaches to enhancing the representativeness of samples. But research is a community effort, to be shared whenever possible; studies of too limited a nature are of little benefit to the advancement of knowledge.

On the other hand, case studies in convenience groups can provide valuable insights and understanding of a scale not possible to find in large more representative samples. Available groups for case studies overcome the problem of the very large resources needed to collect the same amount of data from a larger representative sample. The limitations of such studies are that it is more difficult to justify extending the results and conclusions to larger populations. This is a continual dilemma for researchers, whether their results will be of sufficient depth (the question of social science significance) and not trivial, and at the same time have some level of generalizability. If care is taken, studies employing the two extremes, small samples studied in depth and large samples where only a few variables are investigated, can complement each other. This is where it is the responsibility of the researcher to ensure through a literature search that his or her study builds upon that of others. This is true at both extremes: the in-depth study of a small sample can have its generalizability enhanced if some of the relevant variables have been investigated on a larger, more representative scale; the large representative study covering a few variables can have its relative academic significance enhanced through building upon other research, in particular localized studies that have found results whose generalizability is in question. Often, on their own and carried out in isolation, the two types of studies can produce sterile results. Since few researchers have the resources to study comprehensively an issue as thoroughly as they would like, it becomes the collective responsibility of the research community to ensure that the links are there through literature searches.

Criteria for evaluating representativeness

Defined below are the criteria for judging the relative representativeness of a sample, an expansion of the second column in the Profiling Sheet labelled 'Representativeness':

Whole population. All findings will obviously apply to the whole population, with any error being attributable only to the measuring instruments. The disadvantage is that it may well be that the population is very small, for example a conveniently available group. As long as the researchers acknowledge this, and recognize that the population is small, then whatever conclusions are drawn will be very sound, since they will be describing and interpreting the parameters of that group directly, and not trying to describe population characteristics based upon statistics from a sample. (Any claims of generalizability to any other larger group would mean unjustifiably extending an inference to that group; this rating would be the bottom one in this column; see also the last column in the Profiling Sheet on Conclusions.)

Random selection from a specified population. The researcher has appropriately applied one of the techniques described earlier (direct random, random assignment, stratified random, random cluster or staged sampling). While there is no guarantee that the sample is perfectly representative, it is the soundest approach giving the highest probability that a sample is representative.

Purposive sampling from a specified population. Some attempt has been made to select a representative sample through specific criteria or characteristics related to variables that are to be controlled. This is not the best way of choosing a sample, but better than the next.

Volunteers. This level will include quota, accidental, convenience and snowball sampling, as described above. While there is some endeavour to obtain a sample that could be considered representative, such a sample is not very convincing. There is also the situation where the researcher starts with a random sample, but ends up with volunteers from the group selected (thus you may want to circle *both*). The key to justifying a high level of representativeness in this situation is for the researcher to have found out why those who dropped out did not choose to participate. Ideally, the researcher should show that neither the way the study was conducted nor the variables investigated had anything to do with non-participation.

Unidentified group. The description of the sample or the sampling technique is not sufficiently clear either to indicate the population or to justify any generalizability to a population. Alternatively, the claim of generalizability is simply unjustifiable!

Finally, use your new skills on evaluating representativeness with Activity 3.5.

Activity 3.5

Select several articles and evaluate them using the criteria in the columns of the Profiling Sheet given at the end of this chapter. This includes those for the Questions/hypotheses column, as well as the new ones for Representativeness. Note that it is worthwhile choosing at least one new article each time to allow you to apply the preceding criteria to a new paper.

References

Blum, M.L. and Foos, P.W. (1986) *Data Gathering: Experimental Methods Plus*. Harper & Row.

Chase, C.I. (1985) *Elementary Statistical Procedures*, 3rd edn. McGraw-Hill.

Cohen, L. and Manion, L. (1989) *Research Methods in Education*, 3rd edn. Routledge.

Guba, E.G. (1978) *Towards a Naturalistic Inquiry in Educational Evaluation*. Monograph 8, Center for Study of Evaluation, UCLA.

Kerlinger, F.N. (1986) *Foundations of Behavioral Research*, 3rd edn. Holt, Rinehart & Winston.

Moore, D.S. (1991) *Statistics: Concepts and Controversies*, 3rd edn. W.H. Freeman.

Open University (1973) *Methods of Educational Enquiry, E341. Block 2: Research Design*. Open University Press.

Activity model answers and comments

Activity 3.2

1 All persons on the union roll: (a).
2 Young people who belong to youth groups: (c).
3 All teachers in that authority: (a).
4 Unemployed persons by age, though where the original list came from is not clear: (b).
5 All 14-year-old secondary school pupils in England: (d).

Activity 3.3

1 All those who appear on the county register: it began with (a) but ended with (g), and though this is a very high rate, one would want to know why there was such a difference in the drop-out rates.
2 Potentially the 16 youth groups: (h), not very representative.
3 The aim is shoppers in villages: (f), which can be very poor.
4 All pupils in the county: (e) for the schools, though (a) for the pupils in the schools selected.

Activity 3.4

Intelligence: environment is not totally controlled for any group thus making it virtually impossible to differentiate between hereditary and environmental contributions to intelligence.
Crime rate: extraneous variables, events outside the study.
Holidays: uncertainty as to why lack of response, could be unknown extraneous variables that would have affected survey results, like personal questions about incomes on questionnaire that respondents did not want to answer thus missing data (non-sampling error).
Teacher comments: no control of age group which could respond differently to teacher comments, extraneous variable introduced by poor sampling.

Profiling Sheet: Evaluating Representativeness (to photocopy) © Thomas R. Black 1993

Article: _____

Question/hypothesis (Actions 1–3/Ch. 2)	Representativeness (Actions 4–5/Ch. 3)
Valid question or hypothesis based on accepted theory with well-justified referenced support	Whole population
Valid question or hypothesis based on own theory, well justified	Random selection from a specified population
Credible question/ hypothesis but alternatives possible, or too extensive/global, or support missing	Purposive sampling from a specified population
Weak question/ hypothesis, or poorly stated, or justified with inappropriate references	Volunteers
No question or hypothesis stated, or inconsistent with known facts	Unidentified group

Comments:

4

Data Quality

When the reader of a research report has understood the questions/ hypotheses (or inferred them from the report) and identified the population to which the study refers, it is appropriate to consider in greater detail what the specific variables are and how they have been measured or quantified. Usually the statement of the questions/hypotheses includes some indication of the concepts to be considered, and it is not unusual for the actual means of defining these operationally to be included in these statements. Therefore, some of the following decisions about data quality may be made at the same time as considering the statement of the research question. In other situations, the reader may find it necessary to read more deeply into a report to determine how the concepts described in the research question are going to be defined operationally, and any justification of the quality of measuring instruments used. Regardless of where one finds the descriptions, criteria are needed to judge the quality of data.

The discussion of data quality will be broken into two parts: the first will consider how one judges the range and relevance of variables for which data are collected, and the second part will assist in examining the quality of the actual measuring instruments used to collect the data. The issues to be raised in the first part will relate strongly to the subject matter and will depend to a great extent on you, the reader, and your knowledge of the field. It will encourage you to begin to enquire about the academic relevance and the logical consistency between the variables and the rest of the report. As a guide, this chapter will provide you with some general questions you should be asking about the variables investigated in any research.

The second part will be concerned with technical issues related to the operational definition of the variables, including how well and how consistently the instrument measures the chosen concepts. The methodology of designing instruments to measure abstract concepts is an established one, and guidance will be provided to help you identify whether appropriate steps have been taken to ensure the quality of instruments used in a study.

Data quality, part I: which variables?

In the statements of the research question and hypothesis, one expects to find some indication of the concepts to be investigated. The first question the reader tends to ask is, are these relevant to my interests? If so, then the next question to ask is, are they academically significant? The second question is the one that requires some reflection. How do you determine the level of educational, sociological or psychological significance? The answer is found primarily through knowledge of the field or discipline and often ascertained through familiarity with the literature (journals, conference papers, books etc.).

For example, how would you react to a study that investigated the relationship between the colour of a person's hair and the size of his/her briefcase? Very interesting if you are involved in helping briefcase salesmen to anticipate attaché case size as customers come into a store, but other than that, as it stands it does not seem to contribute much to social and psychological understanding. It would be necessary to look at the justification and reference in the literature to make a final judgement, but just because a study produces nice, tidy data, does not make it academically significant.

What of a study that reports on 'the use of the telephone as a research instrument'? First of all, what is the question? How about, is the telephone a valuable instrument for social science research? The hypothesis could be that the telephone is a valuable instrument for research. Is this even a worthwhile endeavour from the viewpoint of contributing to research? It seems a bit like asking, is a screwdriver useful? Considering the operational definition for the concept(s) or variable(s) chosen to be investigated may help resolve the issue. For the study on the value of the telephone as a research tool, how is 'valuable' going to be defined operationally? Let us say the researcher has devised a questionnaire and sent it round to a random selection of researchers to solicit their collective opinion. Does this help in evaluating its significance? Considering the discussion in Chapter 3 on the problems of obtaining a representative sample, a study that endeavours to identify variables that influence the effectiveness of the telephone as a research tool might be more profitable. There are no simple answers to the question of appropriate variables, one has to depend upon knowledge of the field.

Resolving the question of significance should not be concluded hastily and the reader should allow the author of the report to put forward a case. What at first may seem laughable may provide some significant and relevant outcomes. Ideally, the study should offer to make a contribution to contemporary models or theories, supporting or conflicting with them. This goes back to some extent to the earlier issue relating to the statement of questions and hypotheses. Obviously, it is possible to start with a new theory, but even then the intent of the study will often be to provide a justification for displacing an old one, produce modifications, or suggest new evidence to refute an existing one. The reader again looks to the citation of other studies for support.

Related to the issue of significance is the question of the number of variables or concepts covered by a study. This includes studies that have no hypotheses and purport to 'just look for variables', which can result in considering so many possibilities that the results are overwhelming and contribute little to further understanding. As noted earlier, no researcher is going to answer all the outstanding questions in his or her field of research, much less the big one of Life, the Universe and Everything. Often studies that tackle too many variables have started off with poorly defined questions and probably no hypothesis. Looking for variables is more complex than just casting a net to see what gets trapped. The following sections emphasize many of the potential pitfalls related to choice of variables as reported in research studies, grouping them in three broad categories: case histories/studies, large surveys, and experimental/ quasi-experimental designs. Obviously some of the issues raised here will relate back to the original formulation of the research question or hypothesis. One problem the reader may have is deciding which came first: the variables or the question/hypothesis?

Case histories and case studies

Often researchers want to investigate an individual, an individual situation, or small group in great depth, rather than many subjects in less depth, as a means of answering their research question. Blum and Foos (1986) describe the approach as follows: 'A case history (or case study) is a biographical or autobiographical study and report of an individual, group or phenomenon. Case histories of individuals are used extensively in clinical psychology, but they have been particularly useful in research in general. Piaget's work in developmental psychology involved case histories over time, identifying milestones in the intellectual development of children. Subsequent work by other researchers has involved different approaches to investigate the generalizablity of such findings. Educational research tends to refer to case studies (Cohen and Manion, 1989) since it is groups and their activities rather than individuals that are most often the focus of interest. Regardless of the terminology used, the approach is usually an observational one, with the researcher(s) recording events as they unfold and provide an opportunity to record complex events and the interaction of numerous variables.

Blum and Foos (1986) note that while case histories tend to be valued as a means of recording unanticipated events, they are criticized for being poorly planned. Combined with an inability to generalize to larger groups, this approach tends to be inadequate for testing hypotheses, but of greater value as a source of new hypotheses. Due to the non-representative nature of individuals or local groups, any evidence to support a hypothesis describing a cause and effect relationship could be discounted since the results could not be generalized to a larger population. The advantages of such an approach do provide an opportunity to identify and suggest possible relationships, and provide evidence to support further study. The richness of information collected by skilled researchers can be of immense value, whether it be the behaviour of an individual child at home or in the classroom, the sequence of events in an unexpected situation like conflict in a riot or cooperation during a disaster, or the detailed interaction of a peer group or classroom of pupils. The limitation lies with the researchers and their ability to record what is happening in an objective and accurate manner. The quality of evidence and information can be enhanced by employing observation schedules and guidelines to focus observers' attention on important events in what is often a time-restricted, intense period of data collection. The design of schedules has an established methodology and means for testing the quality of the data gathered, as will be seen in the next section. Trained observers with schedules are much more effective data-gatherers than the untrained sitter waiting for something (anything) to happen. The latter tends to be overwhelmed with data or misses those events that would contribute to the research. The reader of research reports of this nature should expect some description and justification of the observation schedule or plan as part of the study. The lack of organized observation can result in missed opportunities or confused reporting, which leads to poorly defined or even omitted records of data.

Large surveys

Data from large surveys can come from at least two different sources: surveys conducted by the researchers themselves and surveys conducted by others, for example census data. These usually consist of written or oral questionnaires administered to as large and as representative a sample as possible. A census usually tries to get everyone to respond to a basic set of questions and then members of a representative sample are asked additional detailed questions.

Survey data can provide opinions, attitudes, intentions and beliefs, but all are recording data about the subjects' *perceptions* of the issues presented. This presents a problem for some researchers in how they report the results. For example, a study which asks whether a particular political candidate is 'honest' and finds that 95 per cent respond 'yes' might report that he or she is honest, but this is not necessarily true. It is doubtful that the public would have sufficient evidence on the candidate's activities to be able to make such a judgement, and therefore the best the researcher could report would be that 95 per cent of the public *perceives* the candidate to be honest. The reader of a report must keep in mind that there can be radical differences between truth and perception. Consequently, a check can be made between what is stated as a question or hypothesis, and what is actually measured, making sure that there is no loss of logical consistency, subtle or obvious. This issue of consistency across a study will arise again in the next section on technical aspects of questionnaire design as one aspect of validity, and in Chapter 8 when considering conclusions drawn in a report.

The major issue to consider here with respect to surveys is the one of the potentially large numbers of variables investigated. Census data are a good example of survey data that provide fairly objective details of age, income, house size, family size etc. The problem with a census is that it is primarily a data collection exercise and is not designed to test specific hypotheses. Researchers scouring census data for ammunition to prove or disprove their own hypotheses may have a wealth of numbers to contend with, but it may prove difficult to make any sense of this gold mine. As if one needed to be reminded, the ubiquitous computer and its powerful software are capable of handling large amounts of data, though not necessarily intelligently. It is quite possible to carry out data snooping, in the form of correlating every variable with every other variable just to see if anything comes out, relatively painlessly on a computer. The pain comes in trying to understand what it all means. Take, for example, the following seven unambiguous 'census' variables: age, income, number of children, number of rooms in home, number of toilets, number of books in personal library, and number of cars owned. There are 21 possible correlations, not all of which mean anything. So what if there is a significant correlation between the number of books in the personal library and the number of toilets in the house? One would hope that no inferences would be drawn about reading habits from such results.

Even if the concepts are meaningful, there is always the probability that a statistically significant result will appear by chance alone. As Blum and Foos (1986) note about such data snooping, even if the level of significance is set at 0.01, this means that with 100 relationships tested, it is expected that one will be significant by chance alone. Extending this argument, if the significance level were set at 0.05, then one in 20 correlations would be expected to be significant by chance. Thus one would anticipate that for the seven census variables above, at least one of the 21 correlations would be statistically significant just by chance alone.

Surveys conducted by the researchers themselves tend to be more economical in the number of variables tested, simply because of the cost and effort required for collecting and processing the data. There are situations, though, where this is not apparently true. While one can be *reasonably* sure (see the last section in this chapter) that factual data represent the intended concepts (age, income etc.), less definite concepts, including perceptions, are more difficult to measure. Occasionally a researcher will try to use single responses as an operational definition of a concept. For example, to measure perception of the quality of television programmes, a researcher might use the responses from the following question as the data:

	Excellent		Mediocre		Awful
Rank the overall quality of television on the five-point scale.	1	2	3	4	5

Why single questions make poor data will be amplified in the next section, but at this point, the reader ought simply to ask, does this *really* measure attitudes in a way that could be replicated? Would a large number of variables measured this way provide sound data? When reading research reports, one should not assume that because there is a large quantity of variables that this guarantees that the research will be of high quality.

Finally, there is the tendency for some researchers using census data to stretch the meaning of some variables to fit their own definitions. Letting someone else do all the hard work of data collecting may seem cost-effective, but the results may not be exactly what is needed. This practice of assigning variables to data after the fact is one that can produce questionable studies. For example, to conclude that people below a certain income are almost illiterate because they have only a few books in the house and do not subscribe to newspapers or magazines is equating possession of printed material with literacy. How do we know they do not use the public library? To resolve in a valid way the hypothesis that people on low incomes do not read would require asking more questions than were in the original census.

Experimental and quasi-experimental designs

The researchers tend to have control over the independent variables in studies employing experimental designs. Thus, the subjects may be assigned to various 'treatments' as potential independent variables (receiving different amounts of vitamins, using different learning materials, assigned to mixed or single sex groups) and the consequences for some dependent variables are measured (IQ, achievement, self-confidence). Such designs tend to be difficult to arrange and are often considered artificial and divorced from reality. Therefore, similar designs are applied using existing groups of people and are called quasi-experimental designs. The subjects tend already to have had something happen to them as part of life (educational background, social class, age group, sex) and the researcher attempts to ascertain the effect of these potential independent variables on some chosen dependent variable, such as learning ability, attitudes, political preference etc.

In either situation, there is not much scope for a large number of variables, since to test hypotheses, each variable would need two or more levels or categories of treatment. As we will see in Chapter 7, to have three variables with three levels each would require something in the order of 300 subjects. To acquire 300 persons to participate in an experimental design would be difficult enough, but to find 30+ persons to fit each of the combinations of variable for a quasi-experimental study can be equally difficult. And that is a simple design. As a consequence, most studies employing such approaches tend to investigate a few, very carefully chosen variables. For these studies, the reader will be concerned not so much with the number of variables, but their relevance and value to research. One criticism frequently levelled at experimental and quasi-experimental designs has been the trivial nature of the variables. The choice of concepts and hypothesized relationships requires substantial background reading and consideration of previous research if such studies are going to investigate potentially meaningful relationships.

Criteria for evaluating variable significance

Defined below are the criteria for the column in the Profiling Sheet for Data Quality I, with a brief explanation of each level:

Educationally, sociologically, psychologically etc. significant and a manageable number of concepts. Your knowledge of the discipline or field will determine the relative significance. The number of variables may depend on the sample size and how the data are going to be processed. The variables chosen will probably be unambiguous, well defined and/or supported by a sound theory and literature citations.

Limited academic significance, very narrow perspective. It is possible to be too narrow in one's outlook and to focus on too few concepts or variables in such restricted situations as to make the results not applicable to real life.

Large number of concepts, potentially confusing. Too many concepts, and consequently too many variables measured, can result in a large number of facts, but no new understanding of interrelationships among the variables. This often occurs when researchers have no clear question or hypothesis to guide the data collection process. For the same effort, fewer variables could have been studied with greater understanding of relationships.

Too many concepts and variables investigated to result in any meaning. Surveys using questionnaires that collect vast amounts of information, sent to large numbers of people can produce overwhelming amounts of data. If the questionnaires are not well designed (as will be seen below), then the study will generate many facts, but little new understanding of relationships among variables. Recycling census data may produce equally dubious results.

Trivial concepts, not academically significant. One of the criticisms levelled at statistically based studies employing experimental designs is that they trivialize situations in order to collect quantifiable data. The study is done in such isolation as to provide relatively little new information. This can happen with survey and case study data as well.

Please now do Activity 4.1.

Activity 4.1

Choose one or more articles and evaluate the relative significance of the (potential) variables studied, using the criteria outlined above. Use the appropriate column in the Profiling Sheet at the end of this chapter.

Data quality, part II: measuring instruments

When reading a report, one looks for consistency between the hypotheses/ questions and the variables chosen. Questions and hypotheses for educational and social science research tend to be expressed in terms of generally abstract concepts, like reinforcement, achievement, success, leadership etc. The general question to be answered here is: are the measured variables good operational definitions of these rather vague and abstract concepts? An *operational definition* is the evidence a researcher uses as justification for the relative existence (sometimes quantified) of the abstract concept. Since much of what is studied is not tangible, this provides a considerable challenge, particularly when there is no widely accepted operational definition for a concept. For example, take the concept 'leadership'. Not only might a study want to determine whether it even exists in certain circumstances, but also it may be desirable to quantify it in terms of quality (rating it against criteria defining good to poor) and quantity (too much to too little).

In addition, it is worthwhile recognizing two separate events that will influence the determination of relative quality of the operational definitions: the actual design of the measuring instruments and the process of collecting data. Each will have a bearing on the three main concepts that underlie the criteria for judging data quality: validity, reliability and objectivity.

There are numerous textbooks that provide extensive guidance on the design of measuring instruments for use in education, psychology and sociology: several of these are included in the references at the end of the chapter. This chapter cannot comprehensively cover such a vast topic, but it will provide some general criteria for judging the quality of measuring instruments employed in research. Reports should provide sufficient background information to judge the level of care taken when designing and using the measuring instruments developed, borrowed or purchased. If you intend to dissect specific instruments or create your own, you should enquire more deeply into the literature.

Validity

Basically, to ensure *validity*, any instrument must measure what it was intended to measure. This means that the instrument, as the operational definition, must be logically consistent and cover comprehensively all aspects of the abstract concept to be studied. Ideally, it should be possible to confirm this through alternative, independent observation. The measurement literature traditionally has defined a number of different types of validity, some of which overlap. The discussion of validity in the literature is littered with controversy, but for simplicity, two commonly defined types will be used as the basis for establishing a working definition of validity for measuring instruments used in research: construct validity and content validity.

Construct validity

This is considered to be the most important for research design, since it is concerned with the measurement of abstract concepts and traits, such as intelligence, anxiety, logical reasoning, attitude towards dogs, social class or knowledge of French etc. To a certain degree, the validity of each of these is dependent upon a definition or description of the terminology. How is 'anxiety' defined? What constitutes 'knowledge of French'? In the latter case, it may be that the operational definition is a score on an examination, in which case, it would be necessary to explore in detail the content validity (see below) of that specific test.

Starting with a definition, one then proceeds to elaborate on all the component characteristics that provide evidence of the trait or construct. The observable, recordable or otherwise measurable aspects will eventually make up the instrument. In particular, this means that it is highly unlikely that a *single* question on a questionnaire or asked in an interview would ever constitute a valid operational definition of anything but a trivial concept. An adequate operational definition would have to consist of a number of questions in a questionnaire (or points in an observation schedule, or criteria for classification etc.) to incorporate sufficient characteristics to cover all relevant aspects of the concept or construct under study (see for example, Oppenheim, 1992).

For example, consider a variable in a study such as 'the perception of the quality of television', and recall the single question suggested above to measure this. First of all, a valid measure would require that the researcher elaborate on what is meant by the term 'quality'. Is there an interest in the reaction of subjects to the quality of what is presented to the public? Or is there an interest in the reaction to its influence on the public and contemporary culture? If it were the former, then there would be a need to obtain the subject's perception of the quality of a variety of types of programmes (game shows, drama, news, chat shows etc.). Just asking a single question to rate television on a scale 1 to 5 would be too vague for the subjects, much less for the researcher, and leaves it up to the subject to define what aspects of television should be considered. How attitudes are defined will determine the wording of questions. With respect to the quality of television, is the intent to determine how much subjects *feel* about television (emotional), or to determine values in terms of information, entertainment, or enlightenment (rational judgement), or is the intent to look for negative aspects such as the propensity for the medium to be perceived as time wasting, addictive or providing an unreal view of life?

Even more widely discussed concepts can present researchers with some difficulty when it comes to justifying the validity of the instruments they wish to use. For example, a well-aired, though not fully resolved, controversy exists over what constitutes a valid measure of intelligence. The first recognized tests were developed in 1905 by Binet and Simon, consisting of 30 problems or tests arranged in order of increasing difficulty (Anastasi, 1990). Since then, there has been a wide variety of tests developed, some necessarily administered by trained examiners to individual subjects, and others that are paper-based and administered to large groups. Even though IQ (intelligence quotient) tests are numerous and diverse in nature, there is a tendency to assume that they are all one and the same, and that they somehow directly, validly and reliably measure intelligence on some absolute scale. IQ test scores tend to reflect a set of abilities at a given time as compared to available age norm groups, usually culturally homogeneous. Contemporary research has identified numerous environmental factors that can contribute to rises and falls in IQ, thus potentially complicating any research conducted over time. Anastasi's (1990) book provides an extensive survey of the issues involved, which go beyond the scope of this book. Let it suffice to say that any researchers purporting to use IQ as a variable in their research should describe *which* IQ instrument they are using, its rationale for validity, and its published reliability. The reader will then have sufficient information on which to begin to carry out further investigation of the appropriateness of the test and identify any potential confounding variables.

Similar comments can be made about most *standardized* tests, those that provide norms for a representative sample of a larger population. Among other applications, these statistics allow researchers to use the tests to group subjects according to traits that would otherwise be difficult to determine. They can be used to justify the representativeness of a sample for proficiency or achievement of some skill, say speaking French, since the group of interest has a mean score not significantly different from that of the published statistics for the test. They can also be used post-test for research to evaluate the relative effectiveness of different teaching strategies, though there would be a need to ensure that the tests and the teaching were covering the same topics at the same cognitive level.

Anastasi (1990) defines another category of standardized instruments, *personality tests* as 'instruments for the measurement of emotional, motivational, interpersonal, and attitudinal characteristics, as distinguished from abilities', and points out that hundreds are available. The appropriateness of any single test for research will need to be justified by the researchers in some detail, and not just on the basis of a title or brief description. Most are used primarily for clinical practice and counselling, and tend not to be used in isolation as research instruments.

When reading a report of a study that has developed its own measuring instrument, what does one expect for the justification for construct validity of that instrument? This could be achieved by having the instrument reviewed and evaluated for validity by other experts in the field. Alternatively, the traits to be observed might be sufficiently obvious or unambiguous that justification could be accomplished through reference to the literature. Finally, Anastasi (1990) and Cronbach (1990) maintain that the following three types of validity only expand upon the meaning of construct validity and help to focus our attention on contributing characteristics that may depend upon the nature of the concepts to be defined.

First, *criterion-related validity* can be checked by comparing the data against an alternative set of data. There are two ways of establishing criterion-related validity, depending primarily on the function of the test (Anastasi, 1990), which are best clarified through examples. Consider the situation where it is necessary to check the validity of an instrument constructed to predict mathematical success: a set of results could be compared to the subjects' success in subsequent national mathematics examinations. Alternatively, results on a post-test of a training course could be validated by comparing them to on-the-job performance of the tested skills. Both of these would be also checks of *predictive validity*, how well they predict future performance. So why even have the test if you are going to check up on the subjects later? Standardized aptitude tests are often used as predictors of future success or in identifying potential to learn. In research, this approach is used only on a representative sample of subjects in the population to confirm the criterion-related validity of an instrument to be used on another, possibly larger, sample.

The second form is best illustrated by considering the relationship between the results of a test of arithmetic ability and the independent assessment of a supervisor, like a report that Bloggs continually makes errors in addition. The potential function of this test is to diagnose, not predict, thus the check is on its *concurrent validity*. The validity of the test is based upon knowing the present condition of a sample of examinees or subjects.

The expectations of the reader evaluating research are straightforward: a report claiming that an instrument has criterion-related validity should have carried out a process of confirmation, or used an instrument for which the criterion-related validity has already been established. For example, several studies have been carried out in Britain investigating the relationship between students' A-level examination results (taken by 18+ year-olds and approximately equivalent in content coverage and depth to first-year American university subjects) and the classification of subsequently acquired degrees (roughly equivalent to classifying degrees on the basis of grade-point averages in some higher education systems). It has been shown that for all subjects there were statistically significant correlations between A-level grades and subsequent degree classification; they probably did not occur by chance alone, *but* the correlations (which are sometimes referred to as coefficients of predictive validity) were always low, never more than 0.40 and often of the order of 0.20 (Bourner and Hamad, 1987). Since these correlations indicate the degree of accuracy in predicting degree results from A-level examination results and could range from 0.00 (never an accurate prediction) to 1.00 (perfect prediction every time), this is not very high. In other words, many of those who received low passes (D and

E) at A-level did very well (IIi and First) in degree courses, while many of those receiving high passes at A-level did less well subsequently (IIii and Third). This means that the validity of using A-level grades to predict high achievers in higher education is very low. This type of study does not, unfortunately, seem to dissuade many university selectors in Britain from admitting to their courses only students with high A-level grades.

Content validity

This applies to validating the content of an achievement test or qualifying examination. This might be carried out by comparing the topic coverage and cognitive emphasis of an examination to the original specifications in a syllabus. Examination boards and organizations that produce standardized tests tend to be very meticulous about such processes, while classroom teachers lack the resources and usually collect questions for tests less systematically. If scores on a test or examination constitute an operational definition of 'competency in a subject', the reader will expect some indication of independent verification that the test content was consistent with a syllabus or some other form of agreed content specification. Obviously the problem is that any test will contain only a representative sample of the possible questions that could be asked about a subject. Therefore, to ensure content validity, there need to be questions that are representative of the cognitive emphasis required by the subject (ranging from remembering facts to solving new and unique problems) as well as the variety of content topics. As an alternative to using an accepted syllabus or content list, researchers have been known to define the content of an achievement test and then have this confirmed by other experts in the field. Thus if a project intended to determine if there were different levels of achievement in (say) a university genetics course for different sets of learning resources, then the content of the achievement test used would need to be verified and even changed, possibly on the recommendations of a panel of teachers of genetics.

In summary, establishing content validity is as important as establishing construct validity for aptitude tests or selection instruments (predictive), or diagnostic instruments (concurrent). One problem that does occur is that some tests will possibly have a high content validity, for example the A-level examinations, but a low predictive validity. Thus the use of the results must be considered when considering which form(s) of validity are relevant to a study. In other words, it may be valid to use A-level mathematics results as an indicator of possession of certain mathematical skills (high content validity), but not valid to use them to select for another learning programme (low predictive validity). Reality is such that it is too expensive to make up new and valid selection examinations, so employers and higher education institutions just use existing certification examination results with high content validity to predict success in new endeavours. Construct validity particularly applies to abstract concepts and constructs as used in research, for example when trying to quantify characteristics such as attitudes, personality traits, intelligence, creativity, and the like. Thus A-level physics grades may have high content validity, but without supporting evidence, there is no reason to assume that they are valid indicators of intelligence (construct validity). If it were shown that there was a high correlation between IQ test scores and A-level physics grades, then assuming the IQ test had high construct validity, there would be *some* validity in saying that someone with a high A-level score was intelligent, but no comment could be made about someone who did not do physics. One must always remember that *the relative validity of an instrument is going to be determined by the intended use of the results in the research.*

Before turning to the second criterion for judging data quality – reliability – please consider Activities 4.2 and 4.3.

Activity 4.2

Validity is an issue not only in formal research, but in everyday life. Two interesting sources of examples of operational definitions are newspaper editorials and politicians' speeches, particularly when they include statistics as part of their argument. What constitutes being 'unemployed'? How is the rate of inflation calculated? How are ratings of television programmes determined? What makes a person 'lower' or 'upper' class? Who are the 'workers'?

Read an editorial, the account of a speech or listen to a speech, and identify operational definitions used for specific constructs or concepts. Are they valid? Can you even tell if they are valid and if not, how might you find out? What type of validity is important in that specific case?

Reliability

In simple terms, high reliability means that if you measure something today with your instrument, you should get very much the same results some other time (10 minutes from now, tomorrow, next week), assuming that what or who you are measuring has not changed. An instrument with low reliability is like an elastic ruler used to measure a room for a carpet: you are unlikely to get what you want for a fit! Measuring human characteristics with an instrument that is valid but not reliable will produce potentially different results on different occasions. It is interesting to note that while it is possible to have an instrument that is valid but not reliable, an instrument that is not valid will never be reliable. To put this in terms pertinent to the design of measuring instruments in the social sciences, the following succinct definition provided by Mehrens and Lehmann (1984) is

---

Activity 4.3

Listed below are three constructs, each having three possible operational definitions. Rank order each set as to validity and note why you have chosen this order *before* consulting the model answers and comments at the end of the chapter. None of the choices is perfect and you should try to identify even better ones.

1 *Successful person*
   (a) personal annual income,
   (b) attitude towards job and career,
   (c) investment portfolio (stocks, bank accounts, house value etc.)
2 *Effective teacher*
   (a) success rate of teacher's class(es) on national examinations (e.g. General Certificate in Secondary Education (GCSE) in Britain, Scholastic Aptitude Tests (SAT) in America),
   (b) score on a self-evaluation form covering aspects of self-perception of success,
   (c) average score on teacher-evaluation forms completed by students.
3 *Quality of long-term memory*
   (a) number of nonsense syllables remembered after two weeks,
   (b) how often one wins at the game Trivial Pursuit,
   (c) score on standardized IQ test.

(Consider attitude measures and forms to have been designed, validated and tested by external researchers.)

---

most appropriate: 'Reliability can be defined as the degree of consistency between two measures of the same thing.'

The 'two measures' can mean a variety of combinations, for example: two different tests or measuring instruments, two halves of the same test, the same test or instrument applied on two occasions, two scorers using the same observation schedule, a set of essay scripts marked on two separate days. Reliability coefficients for measuring instruments will give a relative indication of an instrument's reliability, usually on a scale of 0.00 (not at all reliable) to 1.00 (perfectly reliable). Since nothing is perfect, most reliability values for instruments fall somewhere in between. Just how reliable an instrument will be will influence the strength of any conclusions drawn by a study.

To illustrate reliability, we shall carry out a little experiment using a simple physical measuring instrument, only because it is easier to make and use at short notice than a more complex one for an abstract social science concept (see Activity 4.4 on p. 74).

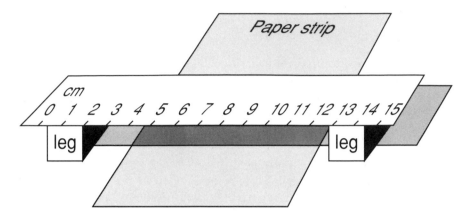

Figure 4.1 *A legged ruler for Activity 4.4.*

Activity 4.4

You need to have a clear plastic 15 cm (or 6 inch) ruler, two rectangular rubber erasers at least 1 cm thick and some tape. Tape the erasers to one side of the rule at opposite ends to give it 'legs', as shown in Figure 4.1.

Now take a piece of paper and cut a strip roughly 10 cm wide (do *not* draw lines with a rule, this must be a freehand cut strip). First make 10 meas·.res of the width of the paper with the legged ruler and write them down (do not expect the widths to be all the same). Make these at various places along the strip. Take the erasers off the rule and with the legless instrument, make and record another 10 measures of the width (again, they will not all be the same but possibly closer together). Find the arithmetic average, or *mean* value of each set of 10 measures. For example, if your measures were as follows

10.1	
10.3	mean = $\dfrac{\text{total of all measures}}{\text{number of measures}}$
10.0	
9.8	
10.1	$= \dfrac{101.0}{10}$
10.4	
9.9	
9.9	mean = 10.1 cm
10.3	
<u>10.2</u>	Keep *your* two main values, you will use
101.0	them in Activity 4.5.

All measuring instruments, whether for physical objects or abstract concepts, will produce a variety of values when applied. This variation in scores or values is called *variability*. In a group of subjects there is going to be a variety of scores on a test, a variety of heights, a variety of attitudes. All the measures of the strip of paper were not the same in Activity 4.4. Even if you had cut the lines very carefully using a ruler, it would be possible to find an instrument that would be sensitive enough to find a variety of measures of width along its length. This variability can be quantified for a group of measures on a subject or subjects or objects and represented by the *variance*, s^2, which is calculated as follows:

$$s^2 = \frac{\text{sum of all (the differences with the mean)}^2}{\text{number of measures} - 1}$$

This would be expressed mathematically as

$$s^2 = \frac{(x_1 - \bar{x})^2 + (x_2 - \bar{x})^2 + (x_3 - \bar{x})^2 + \ldots}{n - 1}$$

where

x_1, x_2, x_3 etc. are individual measures
$\bar{x}$ is the mean of the set of scores
n is the number of measures.

which becomes very tedious to write out when the data are considerable and is usually written in the shorthand of mathematical symbols as follows,

$$s^2 = \frac{\Sigma(x_i - \bar{x})^2}{n - 1} \tag{1}$$

where

Σ (sigma) says the sum of whatever follows
x_i *is an individual measure i*, where $i = 1$ to n, thus x_i, x_2, x_3 etc.
$\bar{x}$ is the mean of the set of scores
n is the number of measures.

We use $(n - 1)$ in the denominator for a sample, but (n) if this were a value for a population. If you take the square root of the variance, you have the *standard deviation from the mean*, whose meaning and use will be considered in Chapter 5. Now carry out Activity 4.5 on p. 76.

[*A mathematical footnote*: About half the differences from the mean, $(x_i - \bar{x})$, will be positive numbers and about half will be negative. If all these were to be added up, the result would be close to zero. But note that after finding the difference from the mean the value is squared (square a negative number and the result is positive) and then they are all added together; so the numerator will *not* be zero, after all (see the example in Activity 4.5).]

Activity 4.5

Calculate the variance for each of the two rulers: the legged one and the legless one. For example, using the sample data from Activity 4.2, where the mean, $\bar{x} = 10.1$ cm,

measure (x_i)	measure – mean $(x_i - \bar{x})$	(measure – mean)^2 $(x_i - \bar{x})^2$
10.1	0	0
10.3	0.2	0.04
10.0	−0.1	0.01
9.8	−0.3	0.09
10.1	0	0
10.4	0.3	0.09
9.9	−0.2	0.04
9.9	−0.2	0.04
10.3	0.2	0.04
10.2	0.1	0.01
		$\Sigma(x_i - \bar{x})^2 = 0.36$

variance $\quad s^2 = \dfrac{0.36}{10 - 1}$

$s^2 = 0.04$

(and thus, standard deviation, $s = \sqrt{0.04} = 0.2$). You may want to try this calculation on your calculator, just to prove it works!)

Save your variances, you will need them soon!

It is generally assumed that most tests or measuring instruments in the social sciences are far from perfect in measuring what they are supposed to measure, somewhat like the ruler on legs. Therefore, we have to imagine that if there were a perfect measuring instrument (like our legless ruler), it would produce a *true score*. What we actually get as a result of collecting data with a test or instrument (analogous to our legged ruler) is an *observed score*. The difference between the two is attributable to measurement error, due to the imperfect instrument.

This error is usually expressed in terms of variability, there being more variability for a more imperfect measuring instrument. Thus for the legged ruler, the variability in readings is due to a combination of the imperfectness of the ruler itself and the varying paper width (remember, there is no such thing as an exact width). In other words, the observed score variability is due to true score variability (varying paper width) and error caused by difficulty in reading the instrument. Similarly, the IQ test scores (observed) of a group of people will vary partly because of true variability within the group and partly because of error in the IQ test itself.

Consider the perfect instrument, the legless ruler, where the variability is due only to the varying width of the paper and not the instrument. To quantify this, we say the perfect instrument has a true score variance with no error variance. This can all be expressed as a simple equation for the variance of the real measuring instrument, the legged ruler, which says the variance in the observed scores is the sum of the variance in the true scores plus the variance due to error:

$$s_x^2 = s_t^2 + s_e^2 \qquad\qquad (2)$$

where

s_x^2 = variance of a group of individuals' observed scores
s_t^2 = variance of a group of individuals' true scores
s_e^2 = variance due to instrument error in a group of individuals' scores.

From this, a rigorous definition of reliability is provided (thus the use of $\equiv$) as a ratio.

$$\text{reliability} \equiv \frac{\text{variance in the true score}}{\text{variance in the observed score}}$$

which is usually written mathematically as

$$r_{xx} \equiv \frac{s_t^2}{s_x^2.} \qquad\qquad (3)$$

Now carry out Activity 4.6.

Activity 4.6

(a) Calculate the reliability of your legged ruler, assuming the legless one produces a 'true' score, since it is a perfect ruler, and therefore has the smaller variance. How reliable is your instrument?

(b) Since the use of the legged ruler is somewhat dependent upon who is using it, you may want to see if the reliability of the instrument is different in the hands of friends or relations. Just get them to make 10 measurements on the strip of paper with each of the instruments and calculate as again above. Also, would the reliability improve with practice?

Types of reliability

In reality, the true score usually does not exist since we cannot make the perfect measuring instrument. This is particularly true for instruments to measure abstract concepts in the social sciences, and therefore the true score variance can never be known. As noted earlier, even the legless ruler is not perfect. The consequence of this is that all reliability coefficients are estimates, depending on what form of reliability one is using. The following are some of the types of estimates commonly reported (adapted from Mehrens and Lehmann, 1984), which are indicators of:

1 *Stability*. This is often referred to as the test–re-test estimate of reliability. This involves administering the instrument to the same group of people on two different occasions. Valid results for the calculation are not easy to obtain, since it is difficult to get subjects to do the same thing twice. There is the possibility that doing the task once will affect the second performance, and there is the possibility of something happening to subjects between applications that would affect the second score. This form is of value for measures aiming at long-term predictions.

2 *Equivalence*. To calculate this involves administering two equivalent forms of the same measuring instrument to the same group on the same day. This approach is most appropriate for tests of content (achievement) where inferences about skills and knowledge at a specific time are to be made.

3 *Internal consistency*. These are really indicators of the homogeneity of questions in a test or questionnaire, or the relative degree to which the responses to individual items correlate with the total test score. This approach allows a reliability coefficient to be calculated on one administration of a test. The most common version of this is the Pearson product moment correlation coefficient, based on splitting the test into two equal parts. If the test has questions scored on a right/wrong basis, the Kuder–Richardson estimates (K–R 20 and K–R 21) are appropriate. Alternatively, if items are not scored dichotomously, then Cronbach's alpha method is appropriate as a generalization of the K–R 20 estimate. There are several other tests available, of varying mathematical complexity.

4 *Inter-judge (-scorer) reliability*. This is highly appropriate for activities where personal judgement is involved, where checking the consistency of observations when several observers are collecting data is required, or to determine the consistency of classification skills across researchers. Data collecting activities like marking essays, classifying test items according to cognitive emphasis or judging a dog show are also typical. For example, if a researcher were recording types of teacher–learner interaction in a class, then to confirm consistency in classification of the types of activity it would be desirable to have two or more other equally qualified persons carry out a classification of a given

class (on video tape) and determine the consistency across researchers. This estimate requires scoring by another (or more) independent judge of a sample of subjects. The correlation between the judges gives an estimate of reliability.

5   *Intra-judge (-scorer) reliability.* This is of value when considerable data have been collected over a period of time by a researcher and the consistency of observations or classifications should be checked. A sample (randomly selected) set of observations is repeated at a later date and the reliability calculated.

As noted earlier, numerous textbooks will provide guidelines for the design of measuring instruments that will assist in maintaining a high reliability. These include the more obvious rules, such as when designing a questionnaire that is the operational definition of a concept, the greater the number of questions that constitute a definition, the more reliable that concept's measurement will be. All too often, single attitude questions on a questionnaire are used as an operational definition of individual abstract concepts, resulting in highly unreliable data. This, unfortunately, is encouraged by the fact that computer programs will take individual responses to questions and process them as if they were scores on a set of questions. There is nothing to stop a researcher from doing this, since the computer will not know any better.

Take the example used earlier, where one of the variables to be investigated in a study was perception of the quality of television. The response to the direct instruction 'Rank the overall quality of television on the five-point scale' might depend strongly on which day of the week subjects were questioned. The morning after an evening consisting of a series of second-rate re-runs could produce a low rating, whereas after an evening of very good programmes, the rating would be higher. A better approach would involve asking a set of questions that would enquire about different types of programmes to help the respondent focus on a cross-section of television offerings. Such an approach would produce more consistent results across time and thus be more reliable.

If you are interested in finding out what the resulting equations are for the above reliability estimates, you are referred to standard texts (e.g. Cronbach, 1990; Mehrens and Lehmann, 1984; Thorndike and Hagen, 1977). What is of primary importance at this point is that a report describing research that used a measuring instrument should provide some indication of its reliability, appropriate to the instrument and its application. Commercially produced or professionally developed tests and other instruments should provide such information as part of the package. Researchers designing their own should carry out their own calculations of reliability and report the results.

The recognition of the non-trivial problems associated with developing highly reliable and valid instruments has resulted in complete research projects being committed to the development, trialing and improvement of instruments to provide dependable operational definitions of specific constructs. Others, as you will find, do not dedicate sufficient resources, and sometimes it becomes very apparent when reading the report.

Objectivity

Objectivity is of particular importance when human judgements are involved, for example, when classifying pupil behaviour using an observation schedule, the wording of individual questions in a questionnaire, or marking an essay looking for certain points. Instruments designed so that they have clear, unambiguous questions tend to be rated as highly objective. Objectivity often depends on how questions, verbal or written, are presented to a subject. Even tone of voice can reduce the objectivity in a situation such as an interview or when questions or statements are read to a group. Low objectivity can affect adversely both the reliability and validity of any measuring instrument.

It is very difficult to determine the level of objectivity from a report. To judge objectivity it is necessary actually to see a written instrument or be there to watch data being collected, hear an audio tape or see a video tape, when there is verbal interaction between a researcher and the subjects. Ideally, a reader would expect some mention of steps taken to ensure objectivity, particularly when the intent of the research is to investigate contentious issues. A common example is telephone surveys to determine political preference. Even this does not solve all the problems of data quality, as will be seen in the next section.

The subjects: how well do they cooperate?

Human beings can be perverse, doing the unexpected and almost inexplicable. Very often even the personal interaction skills of the researcher are not enough to elicit valid and reliable responses from subjects. Historically, various polling organizations have endeavoured to collect opinions from samples of the voters to predict the outcome of elections. As a consequence of the mis-prediction of the outcome of the 1949 Presidential contest in the United States between Truman and Dewey, many newspapers announced the day after the election that Dewey had won (based upon polling samples), when in reality he had lost. Subsequently, polling organizations have invested considerable resources to ensure more representative samples since their results, and livelihood, depend on a high predictive validity, one that can be checked! Over the years, these organizations seem to have become more accurate in their predictions.

Then, more recently, there arose a new factor that seems to have had a significant affect on these predictions. The General Election for members of parliament in Britain in the spring of 1992 produced the usual output of predictions, right up to the day of the election. It was predicted that the Conservative Party would not gain a majority of seats in Parliament and therefore would not be the party in power and select the Prime Minister. The predictions were wrong! It was a close election, but the Conservatives eventually had a comfortable majority of 21 seats (down from 78). What went wrong? Introspection and investigation over the following weeks produced the hypothesis that a sizeable number of voters in the samples who were verbally ask said they would vote for Labour, when in reality they voted for the Conservative candidate. Why, one might ask, when assured anonymity would they do this? It seems that the campaign tended to emphasize the point that the Conservatives, who were in power, were supporting somewhat selfish, monetarist policies, to the detriment of the poor and unemployed. Some people questioned about voting intentions seemed not to want to admit to supporting policies furthering self-interest rather than the more altruistic ones of the Labour Party, so guilt generated a small lie. In an endeavour to overcome this anomaly, one polling organization has subsequently used written questionnaires, anonymously returned, rather than telephone or doorstep interview. Time will tell whether this overcomes the problem.

People do not answer questions honestly for a whole host of reasons. Researchers too often underestimate the intelligence of their subjects. There is the story of the man who had a flat tyre on a road next to a mental institution. As he removed the wheel, he accidentally kicked the wheel nuts off the edge of the road into the river. He became very agitated, not knowing what to do next, when an inmate on the other side of the fence who had been watching the events, suggested 'Why don't you take one nut off each of the other wheels and put them on that one. That will get you to a garage.' The man said, 'What a good idea!' thought a minute, and then said 'Excuse me for asking, but what are you doing in there?' The inmate's reply was 'I may be crazy, but I'm not stupid.' Organizations have used screening tests to identify mental problems in potential employees, and yet these do not always serve their intended function. Human subjects are often capable of identifying what the operational definition of a set of questions might be and answer accordingly. If the instrument is perceived as a threat, then the truth may not prevail. More subtly, some subjects want to be overly helpful and provide information that is not wholly true, but they feel it might help the researcher, so they exaggerate, over- or under-emphasizing (see the Case Study on p. 82).

Surveys among captive audiences, like school children, can produce results that are highly unreliable because they were compelled to participate. Numerous reported research projects use students in the academic institution of the researchers, simply because they are convenient. Ignoring the problem of representativeness of the sample, can undergraduates be convinced to answer or participate honestly? Some instruments have been cleverly designed to detect inconsistencies or exaggerations in responses, but this is not a simple task.

In summary, the best planned scheme for data collection may not be as good as hoped because of the fickleness of a significant number of members

A Case Study

There is the tale of the anthropologists who heard of a tribe living in a remote place that performed a most hideous cannibalistic dance before eating their enemy. They travelled day and night to get there and, after considerable negotiation with a tribal representative, were able to witness this spectacle. They returned home and generated several fascinating journal articles on cannibals.

Years later, another anthropologist related the following, having contacted the same group. The report back to the village leader, Henry, after the meeting between the great anthropologist, Farlander Jones-Smithersbothom, and the tribal representative, Fred, went something like this:

Fred: I've just met another pale-skinned eccentric who wants to come and visit us.

Henry: I suppose he will have to be entertained, any requests?

Fred: Yes, he says that he and his colleagues would like to see the funny dance that we did for those 'explorers'.

Henry: You mean the one they described and had us do where John jumps about with a cow bone in his teeth, you kick the coconut that looks like a head, and I wear a pile of sheep guts as a hat?

Fred: That's it.

Henry: That's disgusting. They didn't want to see the one about happy flowers? Who are these guys anyway?

Fred: They call themselves 'anthropologists' and claim just to want to watch us for a while. They must be bored.

Henry: Well I gave old Melvin a clip around the ear for peeping in my hut at my wife the other day, I hope they aren't like him. Anyway, they are our guests and we must be hospitable. Do have Mary make that nice chicken kabobs on sticks, the ones that look like fingers, but tell her not to put so much pepper on them, the 'explorers' didn't seem to like them much. Forget the tomato juice, that didn't go over well either. And do arrange to have the children go off to pick fruit, I wouldn't want them to see such a degrading spectacle.

of the sample. Sometimes this is avoidable through sufficient insight into the characteristics of the sample and how the instrument will be perceived. Such problems do emphasize the need for researchers to be very sensitive about how data are collected.

Criteria for evaluating validity, reliability and objectivity

Criteria for Data Quality II in the Profiling Sheet are:

Commercially produced and tested with high validity, reliability, and objectivity (V, R, O). Commercially produced tests that are sold usually have published values for reliability and strong rationale for their validity.

It is up to the researcher to justify the use (validity) for the situation at hand.

Project produced and tested with high V, R, O. If the research project has designed an instrument, ideally the researcher(s) will have gone to the trouble of assuring the validity and enhancing the reliability through trials, plus appropriate coefficients will be presented in the paper.

Commercially or project produced with moderate V, R, O. This level is for instruments that have published coefficients that are not terribly high, but at least the values and justification have been produced.

Commercially or project produced with low V, R, O or no information provided. Occasionally, a report does not justify or defend the validity and objectivity, and/or produce any indication of the reliability of the instrument(s).

Inappropriate instrument for this application. This judgement may require some detailed knowledge or experience of the actual instrument, but it does happen that researchers do not use appropriate instruments.

Finally, do Activity 4.7.

Activity 4.7

In the light of the above discussions, evaluate two or more articles or reports using the criteria in the Profiling Sheet at the end of the chapter. You may want to use new articles or ones used for Activities in previous chapters. Photocopy the portion of the Profiling Sheet as needed.

References

Anastasi, A. (1990) *Psychological Testing*, 6th edn. Collier-Macmillan.

Blum, M.L. and Foos, P.W. (1986) *Data Gathering: Experimental Methods Plus*. Harper & Row.

Bourner, T. and Hamad, M. (1987) *Entry Qualifications and Degree Performance*. London, CNAA.

Cohen, L. and Manion, L. (1989) *Research Methods in Education*, 3rd edn. McGraw-Hill.

Cronbach, L.J. (1990) *Essentials of Psychological Testing*, 5th ed. Harper & Row.

Mehrens, W.A. and Lehmann, I.J. (1984) *Measurement and Evaluation in Education and Psychology*, 3rd edn. Holt-Saunders.

Oppenheim, A.N. (1992) *Questionnaire Design, Interviewing and Attitude Measurement*. Pinter.

Thorndike, R.L. and Hagen, E.P. (1977) *Measurement and Evaluation in Psychology and Education*, 4th edn. Wiley.

Activity model answers and comments

Activity 4.3

1 *Successful person*
   (a) Personal annual income might provide an indicator that changes with time: will they be successful next year?
   (b) Attitude towards job and career: depends on whether the focus of the research is about people's own perceptions which may affect motivation, or some external criteria. The choice will depend upon the research question.
   (c) Investment portfolio, if success is considered best defined as the accumulation of wealth.

2 *Effective teacher*
   (a) Success rate of class: there is no guarantee that the teacher is the only contributor to high or low scores, others include social class, school resources, parents etc.
   (b) Self-evaluation: what is the aim of the research? This could be related to self-confidence, willingness to innovate etc.
   (c) Student evaluation questionnaires are like the question on what constitutes good television: some teachers entertain and keep the students happy but do not stretch them, others get students to accomplish more but induce stress, some seem to accomplish both. This would depend on what is meant by *effective*, a difficult concept to define in any situation.

3 *Quality of long-term memory*
   (a) Nonsense syllables presented to a group allow for control over what might be previously learned, but people do not tend to memorize nonsense, and most long-term memorization occurs within some context.
   (b) Trivial Pursuit may test one's memory within a realistic context, but the researcher has no control over the content and how it was acquired and, depending on the version, the content can be culturally biased.
   (c) IQ tests do test knowledge and to some extent memory, but they test other things as well.

Profiling Sheet: Evaluating Data Quality (to photocopy) © Thomas R. Black 1993

Article/Report: _____

Question/hypothesis (Actions 1–3/Ch. 2)	Representativeness (Actions 4–5/Ch. 3)	Data Quality I (Action 6/Ch. 4)	Data Quality II (Action 6/Ch. 4)
Valid question or hypothesis based on accepted theory with well-justified referenced support	Whole population	Educationally, sociologically, psychologically etc. significant and manageable number of concepts	Commercially produced and tested with high validity, reliability and objectivity (V, R, O)
Valid question or hypothesis based on own theory, well justified	Random selection from a specified population	Limited academic significance, very narrow perspective	Project produced and tested with high V, R, O
Credible question/ hypothesis but alternatives possible, or too extensive/global, or support missing	Purposive sampling from a specified population	Large number of concepts, potentially confusing	Commercially or project produced with moderate V, R, O
Weak question/ hypothesis, or poorly stated, or justified with inappropriate references	Volunteers	Too many concepts and variables investigated to result in any meaning	Commercially or project produced with low V, R, O or no information provided
No question or hypothesis stated, or inconsistent with known facts	Unidentified group	Trivial concepts, not academically significant	Inappropriate instrument for this application

Comments:

5

Descriptive Statistics

The term *statistics* usually conjures up a vision of great tables of numbers. What we want to consider here is not the collection of numerical data, but how these data will be presented to a reader of a report which it is hoped will enhance the meaning of the data collected. There are two types of statistical procedure that can be employed, the choice being dependent upon the function or use of the statistics. Procedures that describe a set of data for a group to provide enlightenment on the characteristics of that group alone are referred to as *descriptive* methods. Translating tables of relatively meaningless numbers into forms that actually provide some information about a group requires the employment of a variety of techniques; a number of these will be examined in this chapter. Alternatively, there are other techniques that are used to make inferences about larger groups (populations) based upon the data collected on the identified sample; these are referred to as *inferential* procedures (Chase, 1985), which will be introduced in Chapter 6.

There is a certain amount of satisfaction in having collected data and having lists of numbers, but even mathematicians do not get much joy out of just looking at piles of figures. In the world of computers, raw numbers are referred to as *data*, with the implication that they lack any intrinsic meaning. Processing the data should result in *information*, something that mere mortals can look at and readily understand. Descriptive statistical procedures will allow the researcher to use the data to provide general information about the group investigated, regardless of whether or not inferences about a population are to be made. These procedures involve intellectual 'tools' to generate carefully organized tables of numbers, graphs and calculated indicators of group characteristics, such as the mean (arithmetic average). But as for any set of techniques, there are rules and not all researchers seem to be aware of them, as will be seen when evaluating reports. Computer software often makes the mechanics of generating tables and graphs easier than producing them by hand, but even these powerful tools must be kept under a tight reign so that they are not used inappropriately.

This chapter will introduce four aspects of descriptive statistical procedures: frequency distributions, graphs and charts, measures of central tendency, and indicators of variability. Some procedures will be described in detail so as to assist in understanding the basis for deciding when they are used appropriately; graphs and charts will be examined to ensure that they are presented correctly. First, we shall look at classifying numerical data in a way that is based upon how constructs are quantified and how the data are collected.

Tables, graphs and charts

Initially, a researcher must organize the raw data into some meaningful form. Data often consist of a large collection of numbers, such as scores on a test or other measuring instrument. In many cases, displaying data in a more organized manner can be done by using a computer program, which will save considerable time. It is necessary to understand what the program does and how it carries out the task, so that what is wanted is actually achieved. Modifying the computer adage 'garbage in, garbage out', there is always the danger of 'data in, garbage out'. Basically, it is not wise to assume that the computer programmer who wrote the program knows best. These are sophisticated tools, but still require the researcher to make decisions, and it is not too difficult to find reports where decisions about how data are displayed or graphs plotted have been left to the 'default' decision of the software package used: the results are not as informative as they could have been.

The most basic technique possible for organizing data will result in summarizing the data in frequency tables, which list the frequency of occurrence of specified characteristics or ranges of scores. Tables 5.1–5.3 provide examples of the major types of frequency data, each of which will be discussed briefly. The type of data collected will eventually determine which kinds of graphs best illustrate the results.

Measurement scales

Starting with the most basic type of data, Table 5.1 gives the number of schools in each category for a survey. The variable on the left, type of school, is considered to be a *nominal scale*, as would be any variable which involved name value only. The order of presentation of the schools in Table 5.1 intends no implication of relative quality and the order presented

Table 5.1 *Frequency table for types of schools (nominal scale) in Bloggsmoor Local Education Authority, England*

Type of school	Frequency
Boys comprehensive (BC)	16
Girls comprehensive (GC)	14
Mixed comprehensive (MC)	20
Boys private (BP)	8
Girls private (GP)	6
Mixed private (MP)	10

Table 5.2 *Frequency table showing numbers of subjects in each social class (ordinal scale) in a study sample*

Class	Frequency
A	21
B	44
C	32
D	55
E	16

is not the only one possible. Even numerals can constitute nominal data, such as postal codes (a table showing how many people in each code area), or numerals on football players' shirts (a table showing frequency of penalties for each player designated by his number). The order of the numerals has nothing to do with the data since they are simply a convenient replacement for names.

If the order in which something is ranked is important, such as shown in Table 5.2, showing numbers in each social class in a study, then it is considered an *ordinal scale*. In such a situation, the order does make a difference, but there is no suggestion that the difference between A and B is the same as that from B to C. In some sense, A is better or higher than B, but how much is not quantified. Ordinal data can also result from measuring instruments in the social sciences that require ranking of behaviour or events, such as attitude scales in a questionnaire. For example, consider the following question:

	Usually		Occasionally		Rarely
Television news broadcasts are informative	1	2	3	4	5

There is no guarantee that the difference between rank 1 and rank 2 will be perceived as the same as the difference between rank 2 and rank 3, and so on. It is like a race, the horse that comes in first may have won by a whisker, and the third place horse may be long way behind.

When measurement becomes more refined, then individuals are scored, assigned numerical values on an *interval scale* with equal intervals, though where true zero is on the scale is not known. Examples of such scales include temperature (Celsius, zero is just the freezing point of water and not a lack of temperature) and IQ test scores. Table 5.3 provides an example of a frequency table (or frequency distribution) of IQ test scores for a school. As would be expected, each interval is the same size, covering the same range of numbers.

The *ratio* scale has equal intervals as well, but zero does mean

Table 5.3 *Frequency distribution of IQ test scores (interval scale) for a school*

Scores	Frequency
61–65	1
66–70	1
71–75	0
76–80	3
81–85	8
86–90	10
91–95	25
96–100	55
101–105	53
106–110	27
111–115	11
116–120	7
121–125	5
126–130	1
131–135	2
136–140	1

something: a total lack of the characteristic. For example, distribution of such characteristics as height, weight, and percentage of questions at a specific cognitive level on a test are ratio scales, since zero does mean a total lack of the attribute. Do not be misled by the fact that IQ test scores (interval data) were originally a ratio: the actual mental age score divided by the chronological age (it is now more complex; see Kline, 1991). It is the actual score that is important and only the unconscious (hopefully a transient condition) or the uncooperative in a population for which such a test is designed would ever get zero.

The type of scale that is used will determine how the data can be displayed graphically and which statistical tests will be appropriate. There is a certain amount of discussion on just how much restriction a type of data imposes on the choice of statistical tests. For example, most inferential tests assume that the scales are interval or ratio, but some researchers (e.g. Chase, 1985) argue that one does not have to be too rigorous. For example, a questionnaire that uses a five-point ranking as in the above example on each of 25 questions would provide total scores that could be considered as ordinal. Alternatively, one could argue that since there are 100 possible rankings, that the total score is approximately interval in nature, since the total score range is 25 to 125. If a research report uses data that have their origins in ordinal scales as interval data, then it should say so and justify this usage. It would then be up to the reader to determine the validity of such an argument in that situation.

Planning frequency distributions

Frequency tables for nominal and ordinal data are usually the result of a fairly straightforward exercise in classification: in which category does each subject fit? Tables 5.1 and 5.2 are typical examples. Frequency tables for interval and ratio data present the question of how many intervals and how big? In some cases, each score constitutes an entire interval because there is a small range of scores, but often it is necessary to have *grouped* data because of the large number of potential scores, as shown in Table 5.3. In such situations, one could apparently group the data in any number of different sizes of intervals, starting at a variety of places, but there are some rules of thumb. Chase (1985) maintains that 15 intervals is best but no fewer than 10 and usually no more than 20 intervals should be used. Outside this range, the shape of the distribution can be distorted and, for some considerations, the shape of the distribution will be very important. Therefore, it is worthwhile looking carefully at any graphs of interval data presented in a report and counting the number of intervals. Activity 5.1 provides an opportunity to see the consequences of using different interval sizes.

Activity 5.1

Make a new table from Table 5.3 above by combining the frequencies in adjacent intervals. For example, the new interval 66–75 would have 1, 76–85 would have 11 etc. Repeat the process to make another table by combining three intervals at a time from Table 5.3, making new intervals each having a spread of 15. Save these, you will use them in the next Activity.

Creating a frequency table from raw data requires a few simple decisions, including deciding on the limits for each interval. Examining Table 5.3, it has intervals of five score points, and the process of making this frequency distribution would have been a simple matter if IQ test scores had been only whole numbers. The researcher would have just counted up the number of scores that were in each of the sets of five numbers, for example if 25 persons had scores that were 91, 92, 93, 94 or 95. The limits 91 and 95 are called the *apparent* limits. This would be all that was necessary to consider if the data were whole numbers or integers, or in statistics terminology, a *discrete* variable. But, like many scores, a calculated IQ test score will not necessarily be a whole number, since it is the ratio of two numbers times 100. Such a calculation can produce virtually any numerical value, with fractional parts of a whole number and are considered to be *continuous* variables. For example, using the old system of calculating IQ, a child of chronological age 11.50 years, attaining a mental score of 10.43, scores

$$\frac{10.43}{11.50} \times 100 = 0.907 \times 100 = 90.7$$

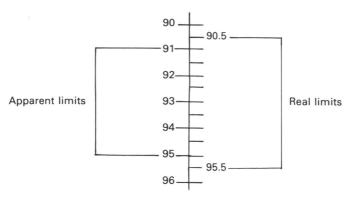

Figure 5.1 *Example of apparent and real limits for an interval in Table 5.3.*

Thus, it is necessary also to identify the *real* limits of each interval, which in the case above are 90.50 to 95.4999 . . . In other words, the interval would be from 90.50 to just below 95.50 (up to but not including 95.50), as shown in Figure 5.1, simply 0.5 point above and below the apparent limits. This derives from the fact that we traditionally round up to the next whole number if the fractional part of a number is 0.5 or above, and round down to the next whole number if it is .499999 . . . or below. The score of 90.7 would therefore fall in this interval and not in the one below, even though it is less than 91 (Figure 5.1).

To determine how many intervals there should be requires a bit of trial and error. First take the total range of scores the study found and divide by 15 (the 'ideal' number of intervals), and adjust from there. For example, the range of IQ scores in Table 5.3 was 64 to 136, or 72 points; divided by 15 this gives 4.8 or rounded up, 5 points per interval. Now it is possible to begin with 64, but that would provide difficult to read intervals since people expect to start with a 1, so it is best to drop back to the apparent limit of 61 (real limit 60.5) and go up to apparent limit 65 (real limit 65.5), then 66–70 (65.5–70.5), then 71–75 (70.5–75.5), and so on. As you can see, $65.5 - 60.5 = 5.0$ points for an interval that would allow the grouping of decimal numbers as well as whole numbers, in intervals of five. This results in 16 intervals that are fairly easy to read, as can be seen from Table 5.3.

Drawing graphs and charts

It has been said that a picture is worth a thousand words, and when it comes to trying to understand numerical data, this is especially true. At the same time, if you want to deceive someone, pictures (or graphs and charts) are quite good as well. To see the true potential for deception it is worthwhile referring to the short and entertaining text by Huff (1954). In this section, some guidelines will be provided to help you determine the quality of graphical presentations.

Most computer spreadsheet packages, like Lotus 123 and Framework,

	Bar chart	Pie chart	Histogram	Frequency polygon
Nominal	X	X		
Ordinal	X			
Interval			X	X
Ratio			X	X

Figure 5.2   *Appropriate usage of different charts and graphs for frequency data.*

and statistical packages, SPSS for example, have built-in graphics facilities. The user enters the data as a frequency table, chooses various options and the program displays (and usually can print out) the graph or chart chosen. Some are better than others from the viewpoint of offering appropriate graphs as well as displaying a high-quality visual representation. Thus for descriptive statistics, sometimes spreadsheets or graphics packages, like Harvard Graphics, provide more appealing graphs than standard sophisticated statistical packages.

Numerous texts, such as Blalock (1979), Chase (1985) and Rowntree (1981), present a more detailed treatment for those wishing to pursue the drawing of graphs further. The most basic question to ask is whether or not the most appropriate type of graph has been used. As noted earlier, the type of data (nominal, ordinal, interval or ratio) will influence the types of graphs and charts that are appropriate for displaying data. Figure 5.2 summarizes appropriate usage dependent upon data type, with each graph and chart illustrated in figures below.

The most basic graph is a *bar chart* (or block diagram), which is used for nominal and ordinal data. It is a graphical frequency diagram where it is the height of the bar that conveys the message. Each bar does *not* touch the next since for nominal data the order of the bars is irrelevant and for ordinal data, the intervals are not necessarily the same size. This avoids any implication that the graph is displaying interval data. To illustrate this, data from Tables 5.1 and 5.2 are displayed as bar charts in Figures 5.3 and 5.4.

Pie charts are picturesque, but not very informative except for nominal data, when the frequencies are converted to percentages. Thus, if the frequencies for each type of school in Table 5.1 were converted to percentages of the whole sample of 74 schools, then one could draw a pie chart, as shown in Figure 5.5. Again, the pattern for the slices of the pie will be selected on the basis of what is most meaningful, since there is no implied order or ranking. Each percentage is a proportion of the circle, a fraction of 360°, thus the area of the each pie slice is proportional to the percentage.

Histograms are special bar charts where adjoining bars touch, thus

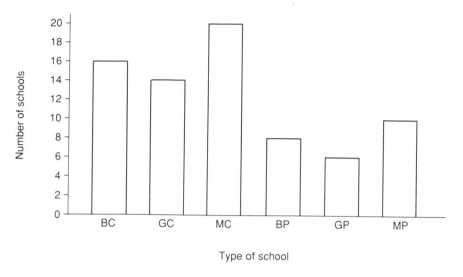

Figure 5.3   *Bar chart for numbers of different schools in a study using data from Table 5.1.*

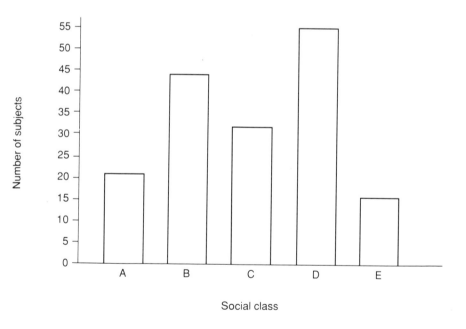

Figure 5.4   *Bar chart for numbers in each social class in a study using data from Table 5.2.*

indicating interval or ratio data, where each interval is the same size as the next and the data are considered to be continuous. The area under each bar, as well as its height, is indicative of the number of subjects in that interval.

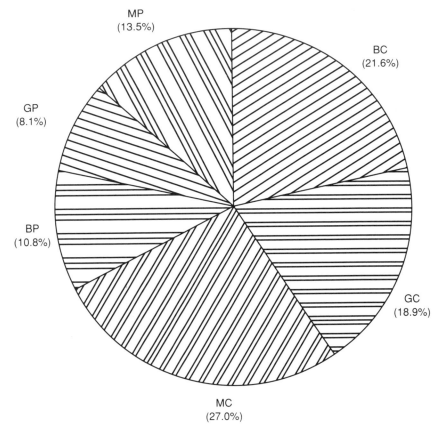

Figure 5.5 *Pie chart showing percentages of each type of school using data from Table 5.1.*

This interpretation for area on a graph will become more important as we consider other ways of displaying interval and ratio data. Figure 5.6 is a histogram of the data from Table 5.3, showing the distribution of IQ test scores for a group of students. Please now turn to Activity 5.2.

Activity 5.2

In Activity 5.1, you were asked to combine intervals to create new frequency tables for the data in Table 5.3. Plot these two sets of data as histograms. What do you notice about the shape of these new distributions?

In Figure 5.6, the intervals on the horizontal axis have been labelled using the apparent limits. Some authors will use the real interval limits

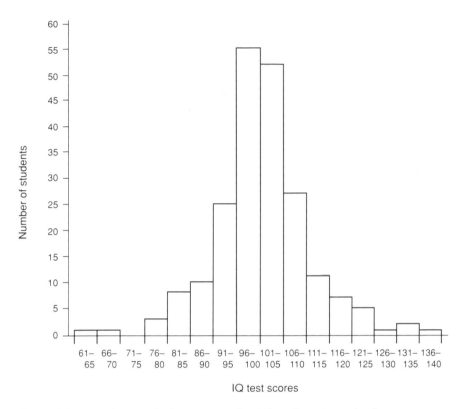

Figure 5.6   *Distribution of IQ test scores for 210 students in a school using data from Table 5.3.*

to mark the edges of each bar. Others prefer to use the number that is the centre value for an interval (for example, 63, 68, 73, 78 etc.), which might affect the choice of intervals. Thus to use the values 60, 65, 70, 75 etc., as interval labels which look nice, the real intervals would have to be 57.5–62.5, 62.5–67.5, 67.5–72.5 etc.

There are alternatives to histograms that make the shape of the distribution more apparent. *Frequency polygons* are just line graphs that join the centres of the tops of the bars on histograms. Figure 5.7 is the equivalent frequency polygon for the histogram in Figure 5.6, and the data in Table 5.3. Note that the horizontal axis is labelled with the numbers of the centres of the intervals. There will be occasions when researchers want to show a smoothed version of a frequency polygon, the implication being that if one had the data for the whole population, it would not be so jagged (Chase, 1985). A *smoothed frequency polygon* is achieved by averaging sets of three intervals: add up the values and divide by 3. Table 5.4 provides the data from Table 5.3 with added columns for interval middles and smoothed data. For example, the new value for the first interval, 61–65, is the sum of the frequencies of the one below (0), that one (1), and the

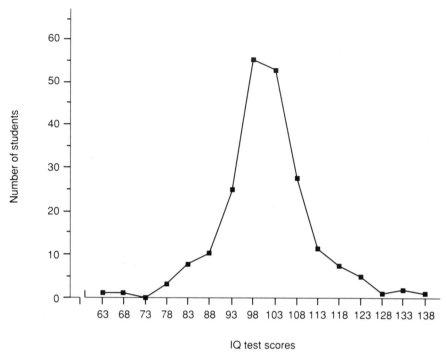

Figure 5.7   *Frequency polygon for data in Table 5.3.*

Table 5.4   *Data from Table 5.3 with interval centres and smoothed data*

Intervals	Centres	Frequency	Smoothed
61–65	63	1	0.7
66–70	68	1	0.7
71–75	73	0	1.3
76–80	78	3	3.7
81–85	83	8	7.0
86–90	88	10	14.3
91–95	93	25	30.0
96–100	98	55	44.3
101–105	103	53	45.0
106–110	108	27	30.3
111–115	113	11	15.0
116–120	118	7	7.7
121–125	123	5	4.3
126–130	128	1	2.7
131–135	133	2	1.3
136–140	138	1	1.0

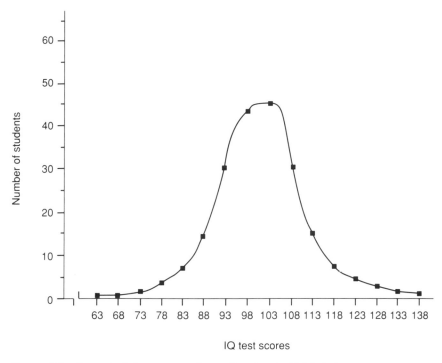

Figure 5.8   *Smoothed frequency polygon for data in Table 5.4.*

one above (1), divided by 3, which is 0.6666 or rounded up to 0.7. These data have been subsequently plotted as the graph in Figure 5.8. It is somewhat easier to identify the shape of a distribution from a smoothed graph. The shape of a distribution is of greatest importance when the choice of measures of central tendency is made, as will be seen in the next section.

Little deceptions

There are a number of interesting distortions resulting from transgressions of the rules that can be introduced when plotting a graph or drawing a chart. Huff (1954) has the best catalogue of sins, particularly relating to the world of advertising, but the few presented here are the most common violations seen in research papers. One that appears all too frequently is histograms with unequal numerical intervals, but showing equal physical size on the graph. More often, histograms are produced with too few intervals. Figure 5.9 provides an example containing both errors. At the other extreme, too many intervals used with small samples can provide flat, uninformative graphs.

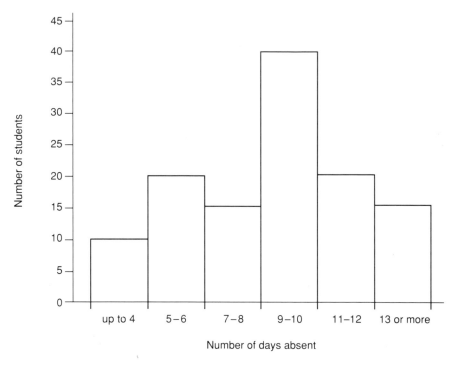

Figure 5.9   *Histogram with unequal interval size and too few intervals.*

Presenting a graph where the vertical frequency axis does not start at zero is an approach commonly used to exaggerate differences. While this is acceptable for the horizontal variable axis (since often we use interval data where zero has no real meaning), it is deceptive on the vertical, as seen when comparing Figure 5.10 with Figure 5.11 and considering the different meanings they potentially convey. Now look at Activity 5.3.

Activity 5.3

Find an example of a distorted graph in your daily newspaper; you should be able to find at least one in either the advertisements or the financial section without too much difficulty.

Characteristics of groups

In order to describe characteristics and tendencies of groups, researchers use several techniques. As seen earlier, the most visual is that of graphs and charts. For histograms and frequency polygons, it is not just the

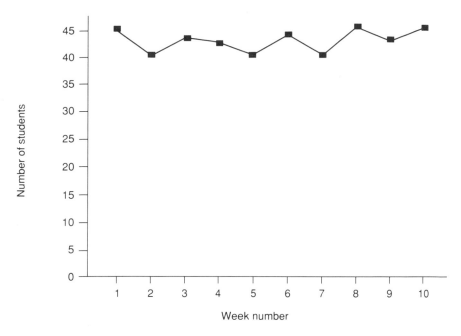

Figure 5.10 *Number of students absent in each week over a term. Does there appear to be much change?*

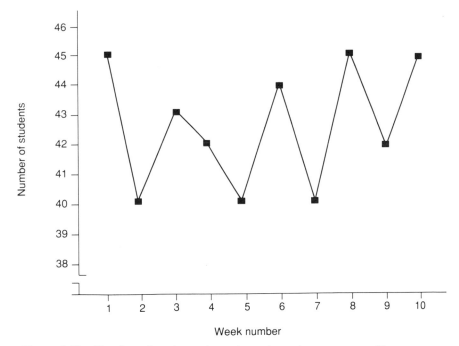

Figure 5.11 *Number of students absent in each week over a term. Now does there appear to be much change?*

immediate knowledge of the height of specific bars or points that is of interest, the overall shape of the graph will also convey important information. Sometimes the graphs themselves are not even provided in research reports, but left to the reader's imagination. Visualizing a graph will depend upon understanding some statistics that tell where the centre is and indicate its width and general shape. First, some common shapes of distributions will be introduced.

Shapes of distributions

Natural variation in performance for a number of human traits will result in a bell-shaped curve, the 'normal' distribution, when data from a frequency distribution is plotted as a histogram or frequency polygon. Recall that this variability was quantified as the *variance* that was a contributing factor in defining and calculating reliability in Chapter 4. A wide variety of human characteristics, such as height and weight at a given age, will demonstrate this variability by forming a normal distribution for the whole population or a truly representative sample. Adolphe Quetelet is considered to be the mathematician who, in the late 1800s, fathered the theory that human traits follow the normal curve.

As a consequence, measuring instruments have been designed specifically to generate a normal distribution of scores, for cases where the designers argue that the trait being measured is normally distributed in the population being considered. Intelligence as measured by an IQ test will provide such a distribution for representative samples of an age group, such as the one shown in Figure 5.12, but this is only because the tests have been designed to produce results that form such a curve. In fact, many of the early US Army Alpha Intelligence Tests (c. 1921) generated positively skewed distributions, with a long tail at the high end of the graph (Dorfman, 1978), such as illustrated in Figure 5.13. In other words, intelligence is *not* necessarily normally distributed just because IQ tests produce a normal distribution. Psychologists argue that intelligence is normally distributed and, as a consequence, psychometricians ensure that IQ tests produce normal distributions of results. It is processes employed during test construction that make it highly probable the instrument will generate scores forming such a distribution for representative samples of the population. This involves selecting questions that provide the greatest amount of spread in scores.

Alternatively, tests designed by teachers and examination boards may well be *criterion-referenced* (actual grades are determined by comparing scores against specific pre-determined criteria) rather than *norm-referenced* (designed to produce a normal distribution with grades based on how examinees perform relative to each other). The design of such tests makes no assumptions about the shape of the distribution of scores and

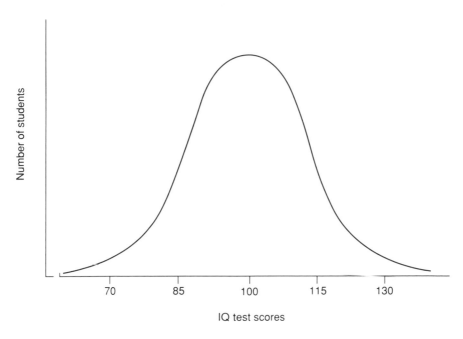

Figure 5.12 *Example of a normal distribution for IQ test scores.*

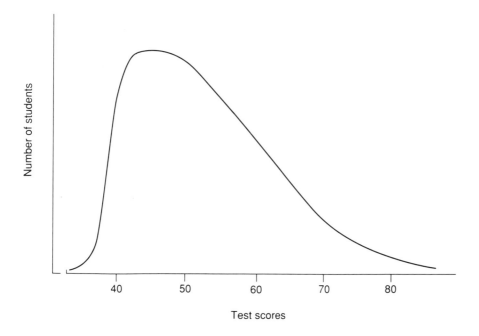

Figure 5.13 *Example of a positively skewed distribution for a measured trait.*

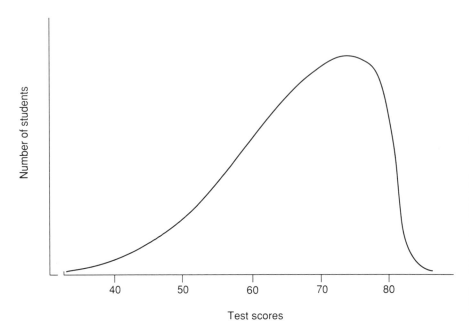

Figure 5.14   *Example of a negatively skewed distribution for a criterion-referenced class test.*

therefore the choice of the questions does not force the shape one way or another. There has been a tendency for criterion-referenced tests to produce negatively skewed distributions (with long tails at the low end) such as the one shown in Figure 5.14. Since the objectives and criteria for success for such tests tend to be well defined and well understood by the examinees, they tend to be better prepared for them, and consequently scores tend to bunch towards the high end.

While other shapes will appear, these three basic categories of distributions will suffice for the following discussion on choice of statistics (numbers) that would best describe a group characteristic. Some other shapes will be discussed later.

Measures of central tendency

Usually researchers use a numerical characteristic to describe a group as a whole, rather than presenting lists of individual scores, frequency tables or even graphs (graphs take up valuable space in a journal article, thus they are often omitted). A number that gives a typical score or measure for the group, one that indicates what the members of the group tended to do provides a means of communicating and even comparing groups to each other. These *measures of central tendency* identify the point on a distribution around which all the other scores tend to group. There are several and

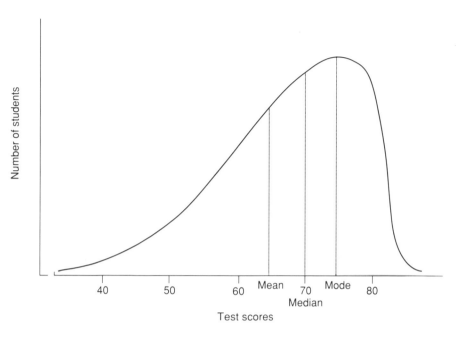

Figure 5.15   *Skewed distribution with mean, median and mode indicated.*

the process of deciding which is most appropriate involves looking at the shape of the distribution, since some measures are more appropriate than others for certain shapes of graphs.

The best indication of how a group as a whole has performed on a trait that is normally distributed (the scores produce a bell-shaped curve) is given by the measure of central tendency called an arithmetic average or the *mean*. This is found simply by adding all the scores and dividing by the number being measured, tested or examined. For example, IQ tests have been designed so that the 'average' IQ test score for a population is 100. The mean is the most appropriate for a normally distributed characteristic if for no other reason than half the scores will be below the average and half above. This definition of the mean is more specific than that possibly implied by the everyday usage of the term, average. Having an 'above average' or 'below average' IQ tells little except that one is in the upper half or lower half of a normal distribution. To say that someone is 'average' is basically meaningless, at least in the world of statistics.

The word 'average' is not very specific either, since it can apply to other measures of central tendency. Another one, the *median* divides a distribution of any shape in half: in other words, half the subjects' scores in a skewed distribution, such as shown in Figure 5.15, will be below the median (but *not* below the mean) and half above. Consequently, half the area under the graph will be below the median and half above. Thus it is a better indicator of central tendency for non-normal distributions than the mean.

The *mode* is nothing more than the score interval with the highest frequency: the interval of the peak. It is most appropriately used for ordinal data, where means and medians cannot be calculated. For example, the shoe shop may use the mode for shoe width when ordering a new variety of shoes to try to sell, since this is the width most people have. For a perfectly normal (bell-shaped) distribution, the mean, median and mode are all at the same place. For distributions of interval or ratio data, the mean or median will tell where the dividing line is such that half are above and half are below, but neither number alone tells much about the shape of the graph. If both have the same value, then it may be a normal distribution, whereas if the median were greater than the mean (as in Figure 5.15), then it might be negatively skewed, and if the mean were greater than the median, then it might be positively skewed. But another value is needed to give a more accurate indication of the shape of the graph, particularly when it has not been provided and the reader has to imagine what it looks like.

Indicator of variability for normal distributions: the standard deviation

When a graph is presented, additional meaningful information can be readily extracted by looking at its shape. The width of the curve indicates by how much scores for a trait vary round the mean and the area under the total curve gives the number of persons being measured. The relative width of a normal distribution, and consequently the degree of trait variance, is indicated by its *standard deviation* from the mean. The calculation of this statistic was carried out in Chapter 4 by finding the square root of the variance (Activity 4.3) and is relatively easy to carry out using many pocket calculators.

Since the normal distribution is based upon a mathematically generated curve, it has well-understood characteristics, such as the distribution of the area under the curve. The standard deviation provides a mechanism for describing this ideal distribution, attributes which tend to be applied to any normal-appearing distribution. In particular, a true normal distribution will have about 34 per cent of the area (or 34 per cent of the scores) fall within each of the first standard deviations on either side of the mean. Thus about 68 per cent are within one standard deviation from the mean, as shown by the *area under the curve* of the marked section in Figure 5.16. Each of the second standard deviations contains about 13.6 per cent and the third about 2.3 per cent. Thus, 95.6 per cent of the area (or scores) of a true normal distribution will fall within two standard deviations from the mean.

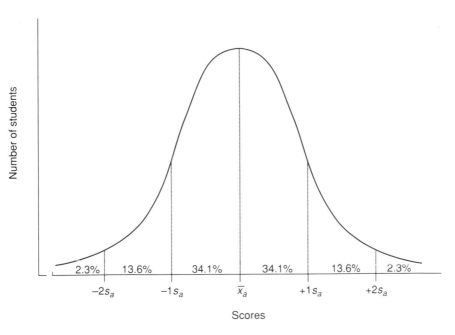

Figure 5.16 *Areas under the normal distribution for standard deviations.*

The standard deviation also provides a clue about the shape of the curve: the larger it is, the broader the bell-shaped curve, as seen by comparing the two distributions in Figures 5.17 and 5.18. Thus with the mean and standard deviation, it is possible to picture a bell-shaped curve with a centre at the mean and a bulge corresponding to the size of the standard deviation. This may be of value to a reader of reports, since often graphs are not provided and only the statistics presented.

Since it is not easy to compare such distributions using one's imagination alone, it is occasionally worthwhile for a reader to sketch such distributions given just the means and standard deviations. Figure 5.19 describes a procedure that will result in graphs of roughly the shape of the distribution described by the statistics provided. Unless the author states the number of participants at the mode, which is unlikely, this procedure will result in a graph roughly of the appropriate shape, but the vertical axis will probably not be correct. This is not very important if the reader simply wants to compare the shapes of two distributions of scores for samples of about the same size, which may be informative when considering reports. You should try Activity 5.4 (p. 109) now, referring to the list of symbols and their definitions on p. 107 as you read and use Figure 5.19 (p. 108):

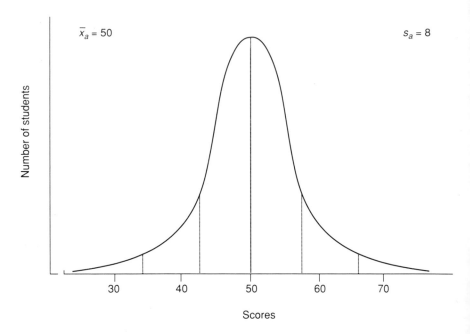

Figure 5.17   *Normal distribution, with mean of 50 and standard deviation of 8.*

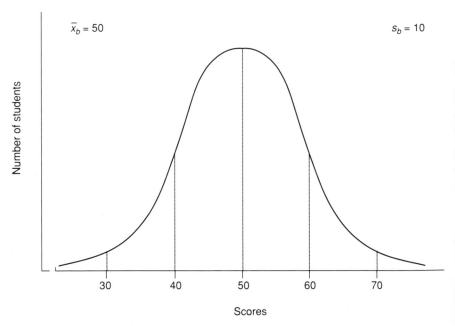

Figure 5.18   *Exemplar normal distribution, with mean of 50 and standard deviation of 10.*

a	=	the sample group designation (it could be $b, c, d, \ldots$).
$\bar{x}_a$	=	the mean score for sample group 'a'.
s_a	=	standard deviation of scores for sample group 'a'.
n_a	=	sample size of group 'a'.
μ	=	population mean score.
σ	=	population standard deviation.
$\approx$		means approximately equal to.

One potentially misleading consequence of presenting statistics without graphs of the raw data is that it is possible to calculate a mean and standard deviation for *any* set of numbers, even data that do not provide a normal distribution. Thus drawing a graph using the statistics as done in Activity 5.4 assumes that the original data were *reasonably* normally distributed. It is worthwhile being aware of what sort of deviations are possible, and ideally authors should describe just how far the real data deviate from the ideal normal distribution.

Diseases of the curve

Earlier, three basic categories of curves were described: normal, positively skewed and negatively skewed. If researchers are rigorous, they will not use means and standard deviations as the measures of central tendency and variance for groups whose data are too skewed. This should also influence the types of statistical test chosen, as will be seen in later chapters. How much is 'too skewed' is an issue that will be addressed later.

To add to the complexity, not all normally appearing distributions are truly normal. Figure 5.20 illustrates what is meant by *kurtosis*, distributions that are somewhat normal in appearance, but do not really fit the ideal, mathematically generated normal distribution. As with skewness, this can affect the types of statistical tests that can be used with a set of data, and the issue will be addressed later. A curve that is more narrow and peaked than an expected normal distribution is referred to as *leptokurtic* and one that is more short and rounded is referred to as *platykurtic*. There are mathematical ways of describing skewness and kurtosis (a perfectly normal curve will be 0.0 for both), but the calculations of these indicators are beyond the scope of this book (see, for example, Blalock, 1979; Ferguson, 1976).

In the real world of research, raw data for a sample may not suffer from skewness or kurtosis, but may have other shapes. Figure 5.21 shows a few possibilities, such as a nearly flat distribution, a bi-modal (having two modes or peaks) distribution, u-shaped, and j-shaped. Like those charac-teristics that produce skewed distributions, these may result from the situations where traits simply are not normally distributed, the sample is not representative of the population for a normally distributed trait, or the measuring instrument is faulty. Bi-modal distributions are interesting in

Instructions:

1 On a piece of paper, draw a line and mark the middle as the mean, $\bar{x}_a$, and three intervals on either side to represent three standard deviations, s_a, with the approprite values. To the left, draw a vertical axis for the frequencies. The maximum of this line should be about 25% of the sample size, n_a, the number of participants.

2 Recall that about 34% of n_a is in each of the first standard deviations on either side of the mean, about 14% in each of the second standard deviations, and just over 2% in each of the third standard deviations. Dividing each of these percentages into *two unequal* parts provides the percentages shown in the table on the right:

19% + 15% = 34%, and 9% + 5% = 14%.

All that is left to do is complete the last column by multiplying the sample size, n_a, by each percentage.

3 Draw a smooth curve through the five points in the three standard deviation intervals on either side of the mean and extend the tails in the third standard deviation intervals, letting the curve approach the horizontal axis.

Example:

1 Given the following values:

$$\bar{x}_a = 105$$
$$s_a = 10$$
$$n_a = 50$$

x-axis scale would be from $105 - 30 = 75$ to $105 + 30 = 135$, and y-axis scale would rise to about 25% of 50, 12 being close enough.

2

No. s_a	%	Interval	Est. freq.
−3.0	tail	75–80	tail
−2.5	2	80–85	1
−2.0	5	85–90	2.5
−1.5	9	90–95	4.5
−1.0	15	95–100	7.5
−0.5	19	100–105	9.5
+0.5	19	105–110	9.5
+1.0	15	110–115	7.5
+1.5	9	115–120	4.5
+2.0	5	120–125	2.5
+2.5	2	125–130	1
+3.0	tail	130–135	tail

Total $(n_a) = 50$

3 This sketch shows what the *ideal* distribution would look like for statistics provided. In reality, the raw data could provide a radically different curve.

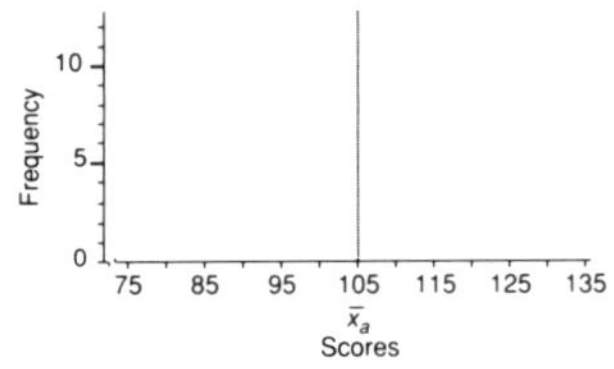

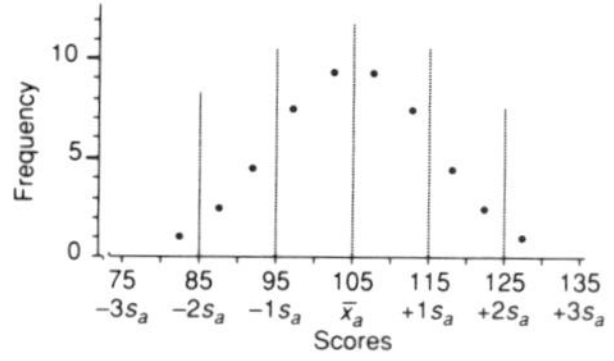

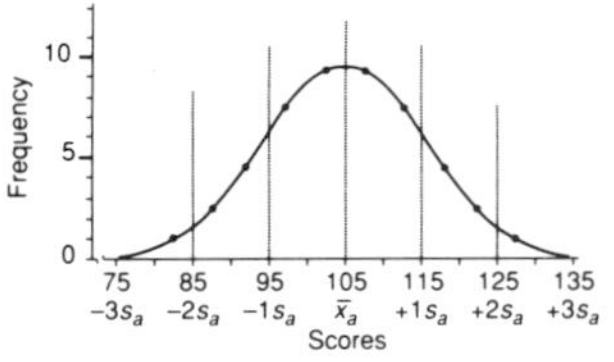

Figure 5.19 *A procedure for sketching normal curves, given the mean, standard deviation, and sample size.*

Activity 5.4

Using the procedure in Figure 5.19, sketch the normal distributions having the following means, standard deviations and sample sizes:

(a) $\bar{x}_a = 101$; $s_a = 10$; $n_a = 210$
(b) $\bar{x}_b = 101$; $s_b = 15$; $n_b = 210$

Complete the table below for each case, filling in the intervals and frequencies for each. Note while each line is 0.5 S.D., the interval sizes for the two graphs will *not* be the same. Plot both graphs using the same horizontal and vertical scales and, if you want, together on the same sheet. Save them, as they will be used again in a later Activity.

No. s_a/s_b	%	Interval for (a)	Est. freq. for (a)	Interval for (b)	Est. freq. for (b)
−3.0	tail		tail		tail
−2.5	2				
−2.0	5				
−1.5	9				
−1.0	15				
−0.5	19				
+0.5	19				
+1.0	15				
+1.5	9				
+2.0	5				
+2.5	2				
+3.0	tail		tail		tail

Total $(n_a) \approx 210$ Total $(n_b) \approx 210$

After you have sketched these, compare your graph (a) to Figures 5.8 and 5.7. Both of these are based upon the data in Table 5.3, which has a mean of 101.02 and standard deviation of 10.3, based on the sample of 210. While your graph may resemble the smoothed frequency polygon of Figure 5.8, how does it compare to a plot of the raw data in Figure 5.7? Graph (b) should look like Figure 5.16. What difference do you see between your two graphs?

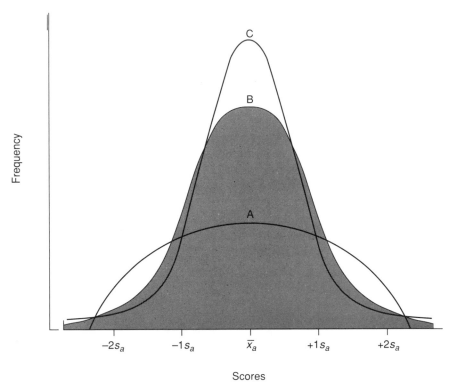

Figure 5.20   *Kurtosis in distributions: A, platykurtic; B, normal (shaded); and C, leptokurtic.*

that they might indicate the presence of *two* distinct groups in a sample, in other words an uncontrolled (extraneous) variable may have had an effect on the results.

Interpreting normal distribution data

It is possible to glean a certain amount of information when provided with the mean and standard deviation alone. For example, as mentioned earlier, IQ tests are actually designed to have a mean of 100 and a standard deviation of 15. Thus, about 68 per cent of all people taking an IQ test should have an IQ of between 85 and 115. One way of indicating an individual's performance is stating his or her position on the horizontal axis in terms of percentage of examinees performing below this position, the *percentile group*. In other words, if John did better than 67 per cent of the other people taking an exam, then John was in the 67th percentile group. If you have an IQ test score of 115, one standard deviation above the mean, then your score is better than 84 per cent of all people taking that examination (50 per cent below the mean plus 34 per cent up to the first standard deviation). This also means that visually, 84 per cent of the area under the curve is to the left, as shown in Figure 5.22.

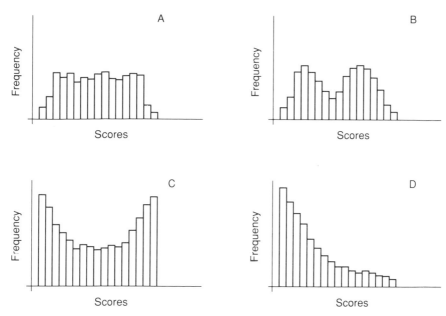

Figure 5.21   *Other non-normal distributions: A, flat; B, bi-modal; C, u-shaped; and D, j-shaped.*

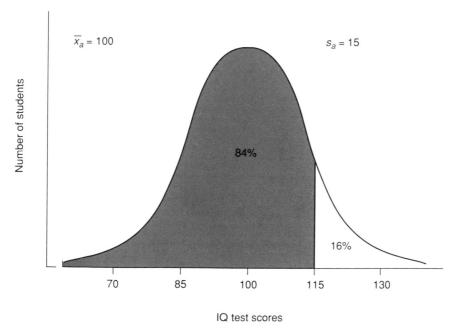

IQ test scores

Figure 5.22   *The 84th percentile group for IQ test scores.*

Table 5.5 *Abridged z-score table for determining percentiles for (area under) a normal distribution (after Chase, 1985)*

z-score	% between mean and z	z-score	% between mean and z	z-score	% between mean and z
0.00	0.00	1.00	34.13	2.00	47.72
0.10	3.98	1.10	36.43	2.10	48.21
0.20	7.93	1.20	38.49	2.20	48.61
0.30	11.79	1.30	40.32	2.30	48.93
0.40	15.54	1.40	41.92	2.40	49.18
0.50	19.15	1.50	43.32	2.50	49.38
0.60	22.57	1.60	44.52	2.60	49.53
0.70	25.80	1.70	45.54	2.70	49.65
0.80	28.81	1.80	46.41	2.80	49.74
0.90	31.59	1.90	47.13	2.90	49.81
				3.00	49.87
				etc.	etc.

It is possible to identify where in a distribution an individual score lies when the mean and standard deviation are known. It is relatively easy to convert a raw score into a number of standard deviations, called *z-scores*, which can be found in a table to see exactly what percentile group that score falls in:

$$z\text{-score} = \frac{\text{raw score} - \text{mean}}{\text{standard deviation}}$$

For example, an IQ test score of 92 would be:

$$z\text{-score} = \frac{92 - 100}{15} = \frac{-8}{15} = -0.53$$

or 0.53 standard deviations *below* the mean. Looking this up in Table 5.5 reveals that the score corresponds to a percentage score of between 19.15 per cent and 22.57 per cent, or about 20 per cent (estimate), below the mean. (A longer unabridged table would give you this percentage directly.) Subtracting this from the 50 per cent total below the mean, results in this score being in the 30th percentile. In other words, this person scored higher than 30 per cent of the people taking this test. This simply tells how a person with this score performed with respect to all the others. What decisions are made based upon such results is the domain of the researchers or others using these data. Now try your hand at Activity 5.5.

Treating diseased curves as normal

What are the consequences of a researcher using the mean and standard deviation for distributions that are not normal, curves that have kurtosis,

---

Activity 5.5

Find the percentile group for IQ test scores of 110, 98 and 120, using Table 5.5. The answer follows the references at the end of the chapter.

---

skewness, are bi-modal etc.? It really does depend on just how far they deviate from being truly normal and this is an issue that will be raised again in later chapters when considering various statistical tests that assume normality. It is of interest, though, to consider just how the basic interpretation of information can differ depending on whether raw data are used or a distribution generated from a calculated mean and standard deviation.

Several years ago, a colleague who introduced an independent learning (individualized instruction) programme in his A-level physics class (roughly equivalent to American first-year university physics for engineering/science students) gave an end-of-year examination that produced a definite bi-modal distribution. Though the original data have long been lost, they were something like those in Table 5.6. From these ratio data (percentage of correct questions), the mean and standard deviation shown have been

Table 5.6 *Data for a bi-modal distribution that has a mean, $\bar{x}_a = 59.2$, standard deviation, $s_a = 18.0$, and $n_a = 143$*

Intervals	Raw data frequencies	Cumulative frequencies	z-scores (based on $\bar{x}_a$ and s_a)	Frequencies based on z-scores	Cumulative frequencies (z-scores)
16–20			−2.43	tail	2.3
21–25	1	1	−2.15	2.1	4.4
26–30	5	6	−1.87	3.6	8.0
31–35	8	14	−1.59	5.4	13.4
36–40	12	26	−1.32	8.0	21.3
41–45	19	45	−1.04	10.6	32.0
46–50	11	56	−0.76	13.2	45.1
51–55	8	64	−0.48	14.5	59.6
56–60	6	70		15.9	75.5
61–65	9	79	+0.35	15.6	91.1
66–70	12	91	+0.63	14.1	105.2
71–75	21	112	+0.91	11.9	117.1
76–80	14	126	+1.18	8.9	126.0
81–85	9	135	+1.46	6.7	132.7
86–90	6	141	+1.74	4.5	137.2
91–95	2	143	+2.02	2.7	139.9
96–100			+2.29	tail	143.0

Total (n_a) = 143   Total (n_a) ≈ 143

calculated. The fourth column shows the z-scores based upon these, and fifth column shows the equivalent interval frequencies that would exist if this were a truly normal distribution with the mean and standard deviation given. Note how the frequencies in columns two and five begin to diverge. This is even more clearly illustrated when the data from the two columns are plotted as a frequency polygon using mid-points of intervals, as shown in Figure 5.23. If one were to use the mean, standard deviation and z-scores to interpret placement of individuals having taken this class test, the interpretation would deviate considerably from reality.

The colleague did suggest an interesting hypothesis to explain the distribution. While the top mode was higher than past means, the bottom mode was lower, suggesting that two groups of students existed: those that actually enjoyed using independent learning materials and those that did not, their attitudes tending to affect their commitment and subsequent performance. An interesting hypothesis, but unfortunately one that was not followed by a rigorous research study. Now carry out Activity 5.6.

Activity 5.6 (answers at end of chapter)

Consider the data in Table 5.6 and Figure 5.23 and let us see some of the consequences of assuming that this is a normal distribution. On Table 5.6, one standard deviation each side of the mean corresponds roughly to the real intervals 40.5 and 75.5 (marked with the larger square bracket ([ ) in the first column.

(a) Using these limits, find the sums of all the real data frequencies and the z-score generated frequencies between +1 and −1 standard deviation.
(b) Divide each of these two numbers by $n_a = 143$ and multiply by 100 to get the percentage in the interval of $1s_a$ either side of the mean.
(c) How do these compare to what one would expect (see Figure 5.16)?
(d) On the graph in Figure 5.23, draw vertical lines at $-1s_a$, $-\frac{1}{2}s_a$, $+\frac{1}{2}s_a$, and $+1s_a$. Visually compare the areas under each of the two curves for the intervals of one standard deviation either side of the mean and ½ standard deviation either side of the mean. How close is the actual bi-modal distribution to the normal distribution in terms of area?

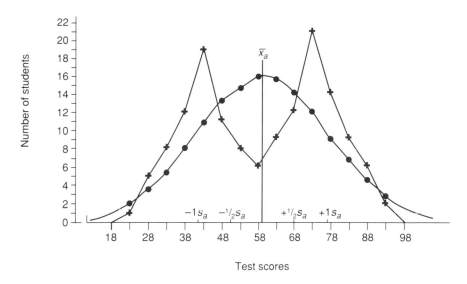

Figure 5.23   *Bi-modal distribution from raw data frequencies and implied normal distribution based upon calculated mean and standard deviation (frequencies based on z-scores), using data from Table 5.6.*

Alternative measures of variability for non-normal distributions

If the distribution of scores deviates considerably from the bell-shape, then the standard deviation would not be the best indicator of variability. Since not all traits or the operational definitions of traits produce normal distributions, then means and standard deviations are not always appropriate. Alternatives, therefore, may be more suitable.

Quartiles are an extension of the median, which together break up a distribution into four equal areas under the curve, each section containing 25 per cent of the subjects. This indicator of variability is more appropriate for non-normal distributions, giving a better indication of the spread of scores and makes no assumptions about the shape of the distribution. Figure 5.24 shows the median and quartiles for a skewed distribution.

The least informative indicator of variability is the *range*, simply describing the maximum and minimum scores for the measured trait. It is appropriate for distributions that have strange and unusual shapes, for small sets of data for which there is not a sufficiently large set of numbers even to plot a graph. The range does not tell us anything about the shape of a distribution, just its limits.

Finally, some studies require only descriptive statistics and consequently present just means and standard deviations, tables, graphs, and charts,

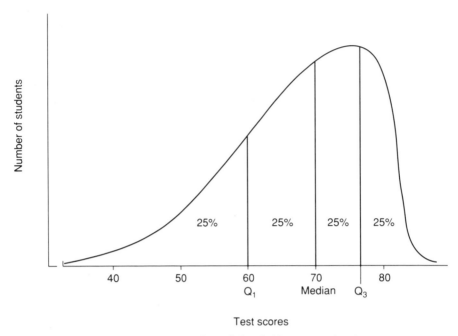

Figure 5.24   *Median with first (Q_1) and third (Q_3) quartiles for a negatively skewed distribution.*

carrying out no statistical tests. As Lehmann and Mehrens (1979) note, a descriptive study is one that is primarily intended to describe existing conditions and not to make predictions or establish causal relationships. Surveys are often attempting to find out what exists in a large population through sampling, while case studies investigate a small population in greater depth. In both cases, the potential problems associated with the measurement of traits plus displaying and interpreting results must be considered. The following criteria should provide a means of rating studies according to their use of these tools.

Criteria for evaluating descriptive statistics

This section of the Profiling Sheet will require you to integrate more complex concepts and ideas when judging a report. You will find that with graphs and charts, aesthetics even comes into the decision. Thus, the levels listed below are related primarily to correctness of use; how effectively a graph or chart is used is something you will want to note in your comments.

Appropriate display of data and results. Appropriate choice of graphs and charts, measure of central tendency, and indicator of variability for the type of data (nominal, ordinal, interval or ratio) and the shape of the distribution of raw data.

Some inadequacies, incorrectness in data/results display. You may want to include just plain poor displays under this level, since most inappropriate choices of graphs produce misleading information (see below).

Other methods of displaying data/results would be more appropriate. For example, using histograms instead of bar charts for ordinal data, using means and standard deviations instead of medians and quartiles for very skewed or other non-normal distributions.

Serious misconceptions through use of descriptive statistics. For example, graphs with no vertical axis zero, exaggerating fluctuations or distribution shape.

Intentionally misleading use of descriptive statistics. By now, you should be able to tell when they are trying to deceive you! While this category will apply frequently to advertising that purports to use statistics, it is not often applicable to professionally produced research reports. Most of the sins manifest in research reports are due to ignorance or poor judgement rather than malice.

In some situations, when judging the quality of descriptive statistics, it will be the lack of graphical representations that will impede understanding. There is also the danger that the substitution of means and standard deviations for graphs of raw data will cover up the true non-normality of the shape of the distributions. As will be seen in the following chapters, there is an underlying assumption that all the distributions are (nearly) normal for specific tests and when they are not, alternatives should be used. Unfortunately, what is 'near enough' is not always simple to determine!

The references at the end of this chapter include some useful texts in addition to the ones directly referred to. These will be of interest to anyone seeking a greater variety of examples of good and poor practice in the displaying of results. Finish this chapter by doing Activity 5.7.

Activity 5.7

Select several articles that use graphs and charts and evaluate them using the Profiling Sheet at the end of the chapter. Photocopy it as needed. Add comments where appropriate.

References

Blalock, H.M. (1979) *Social Statistics*, rev. 2nd edn. McGraw-Hill Kogakusha.
Chase, C.I. (1985) *Elementary Statistical Procedures*, 3rd edn. McGraw-Hill.
Dorfman, D.D. (1978) 'The Cyril Burt question: new findings', *Science*, 201, 4362, 1177–86.
Ferguson, G.A. (1976) *Statistical Analysis in Psychology and Education*, 4th edn. McGraw-Hill.
Huff, D. (1954) *How to Lie with Statistics*. Penguin (recently reprinted).
Kline, P. (1991) *Intelligence: the Psychometric View*. Routledge.
Lehmann, I.J. and Mehrens, W.A. (1979) *Educational Research: Readings in Focus*, 2nd edn. Holt, Rinehart & Winston.
Moore, D.S. (1991) *Statistics: Concepts and Controversies*, 3rd edn. W.H. Freeman.
Rowntree, D. (1981) *Statistics without Tears: a Primer for Non-mathematicians*. Penguin.
Youngman, M.B. (1979) *Analysing Social and Educational Research Data*. McGraw Hill.

Activity model answers

Activity 5.5 (approximate)
110: z-score = +0.667, thus 24.72% above the mean or 74.72 percentile
 98: z-score = -0.133, thus 5.30% below the mean or 44.70 percentile
120: z-score = +1.333, thus 40.85% above the mean or 90.85 percentile

Activity 5.6
(a)   Actual for bi-modal distribution = 86; z-score generated = 95.8.
(b)   Actual for bi-modal distribution = 60%; z-score generated = 67%.
(c)   Expected = 34.1 + 34.1 = 68.2%, thus the z-score percentage is close, the actual for the bi-modal distribution percentage not so close.
(d)   The area under the actual bi-modal distribution is obviously much smaller than what is expected for a normal distribution for $\frac{1}{2}s_a$ either side of the mean, and the discrepancy is even greater than that for $1s_a$ either side of the mean. You can quantify the difference for $\frac{1}{2}s_a$ (roughly) as you did in parts (a) and (b), using the interval between 50.5 and 70.5, as marked on Table 5.6. This simply illustrates the weakness of using mean and standard deviation to describe a non-normal distribution.

Profiling Sheet: Evaluating Descriptive Statistics (to photocopy) © Thomas R. Black 1993

Article/Report: _____

Question/hypothesis (Actions 1–3/Ch. 2)	Representativeness (Actions 4–5/Ch. 3)	Data Quality I (Action 6/Ch. 4)	Data Quality II (Action 6/Ch. 4)	Descriptive Statistics (Action 7/Ch. 5)
Valid question or hypothesis based on accepted theory with well-justified referenced support	Whole population	Educationally, sociologically, psychologically etc. significant and manageable number of concepts	Commercially produced and tested with high validity, reliability and objectivity (V, R, O)	Appropriate display of data and results
Valid question or hypothesis based on own theory, well justified	Random selection from a specified population	Limited academic significance, very narrow perspective	Project produced and tested with high V, R, O	Some inadequacies, incorrectness in data/results display
Credible question/ hypothesis but alternatives possible, or too extensive/global, or support missing	Purposive sampling from a specified population	Large number of concepts, potentially confusing	Commercially or project produced with moderate V, R, O	Other methods of display data/results would be more appropriate
Weak question/ hypothesis, or poorly stated, or justified with inappropriate references	Volunteers	Too many concepts and variables investigated to result in any meaning	Commercially or project produced with low V, R, O or no information provided	Serious misconceptions through use of descriptive statistics
No question or hypothesis stated, or inconsistent with known facts	Unidentified group	Trivial concepts, not academically significant	Inappropriate instrument for this application	Intentionally misleading use of descriptive statistics

Comments:

6

Statistical Inference and Correlational Studies

One way of looking at the human condition is to consider life as a continuous series of probabilistic events, most often having multiple causal factors. Insurance companies actually calculate premiums based on the probabilities that certain events will occur. Thus if the insurance premium for the contents of your house is higher than a friend's who lives in a different town in a comparable house, then this more than likely reflects the difference in frequency of burglaries over the past year in the two areas. Your health insurance rates will increase dramatically if you ski, hang-glide or parachute for a hobby, since the probability of being injured is higher.

On a more mundane level, consider the common cold. What causes a cold? A virus, you say. Well then, why is it that you are the only one in your family not to get a cold when everyone else in the house has it? Whether or not you actually suffer from the cold virus depends on a number of factors, or variables, such as which cold virus (apparently it mutates all the time) and whether or not you have a resistance to that one, your relative health, including getting enough sleep and eating a well-balanced diet, proximity to a sneezer, the quality of the ventilation in the house, the relative humidity of the air (air-borne viruses like it damp) etc. It would be virtually impossible to determine why you, as an individual, at a specific time, did (or did not) get a cold when others did. Other diseases vary in terms of our ability to determine total causality, covering all possible variables. History is littered with plagues that destroy sizeable portions, but not all, of populations. While it is often not possible, nor in the long run profitable, to identify causes with respect to individuals, it is possible to determine *tendencies of groups* to respond to carefully isolated factors, even when it is suspected that there is multiple causality. The difficulty is determining whether the occurrence of an event has happened by chance, as the result of uncontrolled factors, or as the result of the factor(s) under consideration.

What can a statistical test tell a researcher? It can *not* prove that one variable caused another, but it can tell whether the result observed by those experiencing one variable could have occurred as a random event anyway, or not. If the test says that it is unlikely that the result occurred by chance alone, it is still up to the researcher to prove that the one variable was the only possible cause. Statistical tests are like the 'idiot lights' on the dashboard of your car: they only tell you that *something* has happened, but not exactly what. For example, if the *Oil* light comes on, it could mean that the engine is low on oil, the engine bearings have worn out, the oil pump has perished, the signal sending device on the engine is broken, or a wire has shorted out to the light. The motorist obviously checks the oil level first, but if that is adequate then it is time to call the mechanic who will try to find the reason for the light being on. In the social sciences, the researcher should plan a study such that when the light comes on (the statistics indicate that something probably happened), then there are predicted, defendable links or causes.

As noted earlier, inferential statistics involves using data collected from samples to make inferences about a larger population or populations. The complication is that most research involves samples (which are *probably* representative) and involves the collection of data that provide measures of group characteristics or tendencies, possibly means and standard deviations. Using this information, there is a desire to compare groups to determine relationships that will ultimately extend back to the original population(s). All of this depends heavily upon probability, and it is never possible to speak about relationships with absolute certainty, a fact that causes a distinct amount of mental anguish for most people who feel that events should have some degree of certainty.

Thus, to succeed in making one's case in the world of inferential statistics, it is necessary to be in as strong and defensible a position as possible, so that the results and conclusions will withstand the onslaught of competing alternative hypotheses. These include ones that say there is no relationship, or that other variables are the primary cause of the observed effect. Therefore, a researcher should defend any suggestion that a cause and effect relationship exists by undertaking to prove that there are probably no other possible causes than the one(s) identified. In other words, a study must strive to eliminate any competing variables: put simply, there is a high probability that nothing else could have done it. Correlational studies, another approach, strive to establish the existence of relationships among variables that are not even necessarily causal in nature; instead, there may be a third unknown causal variable for two observed related changes, or a common cause for the two observed variables. For example, as children become older, they gain weight and increase in height, though not necessarily at constant rates. There is a correlation between these two phenomena: gaining in height and weight, but one does not cause the other.

The question also arises, is the correlation large enough for the sample size to establish that it is not just a chance occurrence and that the results indicate a relationship in the population? Ultimately, there arise three interrelated concerns that will influence the validity of inferences made about the population(s) and their characteristics:

- formulation of the hypothesis,

- choice of statistical test(s),
- interpretation of 'significance'.

As seen in Chapter 2, there is a need to state the expected outcomes of inferential statistical research in terms of the null hypothesis: that there will *not* be any statistically significant difference. In other words, it is expected that any differences or changes or relationships found will be attributable to chance alone. Even if the null hypothesis is rejected, it only means that the difference or occurrence witnessed *probably* did not occur by chance alone. This probability level traditionally has been set at 5 per cent, which means that if a statistical test says that the probability of this event occurring by chance alone is less than 5 per cent, less than 1 chance in 20, then it probably did *not* occur as a random event. At this level, there is something probably influencing the event(s), or at least the event(s) has/ have occurred as the result of some external influence other that natural random fluctuation. Exactly what this influence is, is not made clear by the statistical test. As noted before, it is still up to the researcher to justify that what he or she did, or the variables identified, were the only possible influences.

This chapter will bring together ideas introduced in Chapter 2 on research questions and hypotheses, and the introduction to the normal distribution in Chapter 5. Before the actual choice of statistical tests can be considered, it is necessary to take a brief mathematical look at what underlies statistical inference and significance. This will be done graphically as much as possible, since most decisions are made on the basis of where means of sets of data are in a normal distribution. Correlational studies and issues related to interpretation of results will be introduced as well. Chapter 7 will continue the review of inferential statistics by considering experimental and related designs, and some of the tests that are used to decide the acceptability of stated hypotheses.

Probability and statistical inference

While it is beyond the scope of this book to present probability theory, it is not difficult to see how the concept of probability applies to inferential statistics. In Chapter 5, the possibility that many human characteristics are normally distributed was introduced. For traits that have such distributions, the mean is the most appropriate measure of central tendency and the standard deviation is the most appropriate indicator of variability in that distribution. There is a distinction made when using these to describe populations and samples of populations: the whole population mean and standard deviation are referred to as *parameters*, whereas these values for a sample are referred to as *statistics*.

It is rare, if ever, that we know the population parameters, unless the population is very small, as in a case study. Consequently, sample statistics are used as estimates, which naturally stimulates the question: how good are these? Just as individual scores for a trait vary around a mean forming a normal distribution, the means of samples themselves will vary if several representative samples are taken from a population. If the frequencies of these means are plotted on a graph, not surprisingly we find another normal distribution. This *distribution of sampling means* will be quite useful in making inferences about the population. Figure 6.1 shows all three distributions for IQ test scores: A, an exemplar population distribution with parameters provided; B, a single sample distribution with its statistics; and C, a distribution of sampling means. The IQ test score is used here simply because it is one distribution for which the parameters are known, since the tests are designed to produce a mean of 100 and a standard deviation of 15.

Remember that when the term population is used, it refers to a group that all share a limited range of common characteristics. In social sciences, these are often not obvious to the casual observer and require some form of detailed observation, measurement or questioning of the subject. So, initially, the question is whether or not a sample as a group is similar

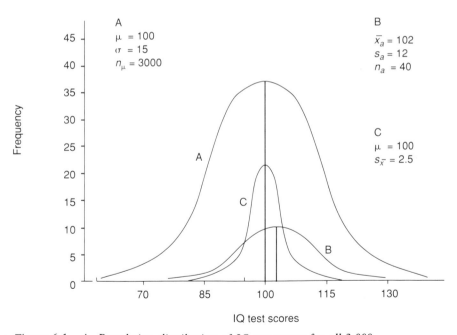

Figure 6.1   A, *Population distribution of IQ test scores for all 3,000 11-year-olds in a local education authority (LEA); B, single exemplar sample distribution of IQ test scores of a random selection of 40 11-year-olds in the LEA; and C, distribution of sample means for a number of such random samples of 40 students.*

enough to the population for the trait or characteristic in question to be considered representative. A statistical test should be able to resolve what is enough.

The first thing to notice in Figure 6.1 is that the standard deviation (and width of the bell-shaped curve) for the distribution of sample means is relatively small compared to the standard deviations for the population and any single sample. Thus it is very unlikely that a truly representative sample will have a mean very different from that of the population. This fact is used in the most basic of inferential statistical tests, deciding whether a sample is to be considered part of a defined population, or part of some other unknown population. To distinguish this standard deviation from that of a sample of the population, the standard deviation of the distribution of sampling means is used, which is known as the *standard error of the mean* (S.E.M.). This will be designated by $\sigma_{\bar{x}}$ if it is calculated from the population parameter, the population standard deviation, σ (sigma), and found by

$$\sigma_{\bar{x}} = \frac{\sigma}{\sqrt{n}} \qquad (1)$$

for sample sizes, *n*.

If an estimate of the standard error of the mean is calculated using statistics, a sample standard deviation, then it will be designated as $s_{\bar{x}}$ and calculated from:

$$s_{\bar{x}} = \frac{s_a}{\sqrt{n_a}} \qquad (2)$$

where s_a is the standard deviation of sample group 'a' whose size is n_a. Obviously, the standard error of the mean depends on the size of the sample: if they are very large then the standard error of the mean, and consequently the width of the curve, will be very small.

It is illustrative to consider an example: in order to carry out a study, a researcher selects a sample of 40 students from the LEA population of 11-year-olds described in Figure 6.1. They are given an IQ test: the group mean is found to be 106. Is this group typical? Let us first state this question as a null hypothesis:

> H_0: There is no significant difference between the IQ of the sample group and that of the population.

In normal English, we would say that we expect that the sample *is* representative of the population for this trait. Here the sample mean will be used to resolve the issue. To make the decision, it is necessary to zoom in on distribution C in Figure 6.1, the sampling means, which is shown enlarged in Figure 6.2. The question now becomes one that is stated in terms of probabilities:

> What is the probability that a sample with a mean of 106 would be randomly chosen from the population?

Recall that the area under the distribution for a range of scores represents

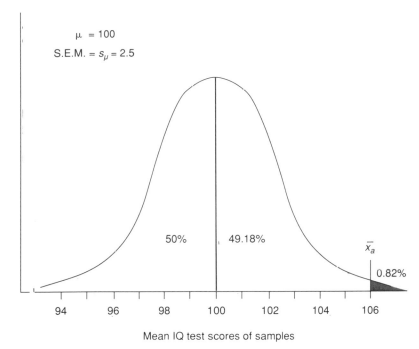

Figure 6.2 *Distribution of sampling means (each sample size = 40), showing the position of a single sample mean, $\bar{x}_a$.*

the percentage of people (or sample means) having scores within that range (see Figure 5.16 in Chapter 5). Using Table 5.5 in Chapter 5, the number of standard deviations from the mean (S.E.M.s) can be used to determine what percentage of sample means one would expect below this group's: here, a sample mean of 106 is 2.4 standard deviations (S.E.M.s) above the population mean, as marked on Figure 6.2. From Table 5.5, this tells us that 49.18 per cent of the sample means would be expected to be between this score and the population mean. Add to this the 50 per cent below the population mean and we find that 99.18 per cent of the sample means should be below this. Stated positively (100% − 99.18% = 0.82%) the probability of this event occurring as an expectedly random event as shown in Figure 6.2, is

> 0.82 of a chance in 100
> 8.2 chances in 1,000
> 82 chances in 10,000

Thus this sample mean does seem to be a highly unlikely event, but what is *unlikely enough* for researchers?

Testing the null hypothesis

For normally distributed traits, those that produce sample means out in either of the tails are highly unlikely. Social science researchers commonly accept that events which occur less frequently than 1 in 20 (5 in 100) are unlikely to have occurred by chance alone and consequently are considered statistically significant. To apply this to a normal distribution would mean that the 5 per cent must be divided between the top and the bottom tails of the distribution, with 2.5 per cent for each (there are occasions when all 5 per cent would occur in one tail, but that is the exception, to be discussed later). Consulting Table 5.5 in Chapter 5, the top 2.5 per cent is from 47.5 per cent onward, or (interpolating) 1.96 standard deviations (S.E.M.s) or more from the mean. The ranges of sample means that would be considered *statistically significant*, and result in the rejection of the null hypothesis since they probably did not occur as part of the natural chance variation in the means, are shown in Figure 6.3 as shaded areas.

Thus for the situation above involving the mean IQ of the sample of 11-year-olds, the cutting point of 1.96 standard deviations (S.E.M.s) would correspond to $1.96 \times 2.5 = 4.9$ points above or below the mean. Thus a sample mean IQ of less than 95.1 or greater than 104.9 would be considered significant and the sample not representative of the population. Therefore, the sample mean of 106 in the example of the group with a mean IQ of 106 would be considered statistically significant and the group not typical, and it is unlikely that they are a representative sample of the whole population, for IQ. Time now to do Activity 6.1.

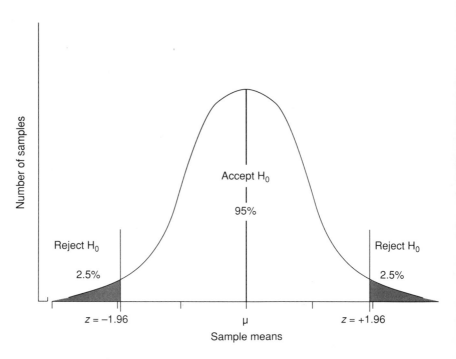

Figure 6.3 *Normal distribution of sample means with 5 per cent significance levels, where μ is the population mean.*

Activity 6.1

(a) Our researcher, having learned his lesson about sampling, now takes a proper random sample of 11-year-olds, finding the mean IQ for the group to be 102. Is this representative of the population? Why or why not?

(b) Our researcher thinks that he can increase the IQ of children by improving their blood circulation through physical exercise. The subjects jog five miles a day for three weeks and are then given another IQ test. This time the mean for the group is 103. Are they still typical of all children at this age? Why or why not? (This is *not* a very good design, but it provides a simple exercise!)

Research errors

Since all of inferential statistics results in probabilities and not certainties, it is not difficult to accept that there is a finite probability that using the above 'rules', it is possible to reject wrongly the null hypothesis when using the 5 per cent level as the cut-off. In other words, there is still a 5 per cent probability that the group does belong to the population. It is possible to make it more difficult to prove that a group does not belong to the population by changing the level to 1 per cent or even lower, but there would still be a finite chance that such a group would belong to the population. On the other hand, what if a researcher accepts the null hypothesis, that there is no difference between the sample and the population, using the 5 per cent (or 1 per cent) level? There is still a finite probability that the decision is not correct and that the sample does not belong to the population. Thus, what level a researcher chooses for deciding is a difficult one and will depend upon the type of decision that will be made as a consequence.

Referring back to the previous example of selecting representative groups of children, the group with a mean IQ of 106 was considered not to be representative of the whole population. While this is a perfectly reasonable decision, it is not proof that they are not representative. In other words, they could all belong to the same class through events not under the control of the schools and may even be the only group with a mean IQ this high. Remember that the bell-shaped normal curve ideally never touches the x-axis and there is always a finite probability that some group will exist quite naturally out in the tails. But the criteria here is that the group or groups selected must be seen to be representative and not deviate from the population group by too much. So, for the purposes of this study, the researcher rejected the null hypothesis and the group. Yet there will be other situations where rejection probably would not be the best action.

As we have seen, if a researcher rejects the null hypothesis because he or she has chosen for a study a probability of less than 5 per cent as statistically significant, then there is a finite probability that the conclusion is wrong. In fact, there is a 5 per cent probability that he or she will be wrong to reject the null hypothesis, or stated differently, there is a 1 in 20 chance that the sample *was* part of the population. To make this type of erroneous decision is described as making a *Type I error*, and the probability of making a Type I error is simply equal to the level of significance chosen. The chance of making a Type I error can be reduced by lowering the level of significance to, say, 1 per cent (i.e. less than 1 in 100 chance, or $z = 2.58$). The less likely one is to find significance, at the 1 per cent instead of the 5 per cent level, the stronger the support for any conclusions. Sometimes this is phrased as relative confidence: 95 per cent confident or 99 per cent confident that a sample does not belong to the population. Also, one will often find the significance level stated as a probability (of something occurring by chance) less than a value, such as $P < 0.05$, or $P < 0.01$.

Unfortunately, this raises the other problem, that by reducing the probability of rejecting a null hypothesis (increasing the confidence level) when it is really true, the chance of accepting the null hypothesis when it is false increases. To accept the null hypothesis when it is really false is known as making a *Type II error*. The probability of making a Type II error can be reduced primarily by increasing the sample size. Assuming the sample has been selected randomly, the greater size increases the probability that the sample will be truly representative. This provides some insight into why researchers are keen to have large samples. These two types of error and the alternative correct decisions are summarized in Figure 6.4.

As Rowntree (1981) notes, resolving the above question is analogous to the following dilemma that arises in courts of law: if weak evidence is accepted, there is a danger many innocent people will go to gaol (a Type I error, rejecting the null hypothesis that there is no significant difference

	H_0 true	H_0 false
H_0 accepted	OK	Type II error
H_0 rejected	Type I error	OK

Figure 6.4 *Research errors based on choice of significance level.*

between these people and innocent people, when it is true). Alternatively, by increasing the demands on the quality of evidence, the probability of more guilty persons not being convicted will increase. This is parallel to raising the significance level to 1 per cent, thus risking a Type II error, accepting the null hypothesis that there is no difference between these people and the innocent, when it should be rejected. Maybe it is fortunate that the conclusions of a single piece of social science research is rarely used as the basis of a radical decision affecting vast numbers of people! How do other professions that use statistics as a decision-making tool, like chemists testing new medicines, protect themselves? They replicate the study using different samples of persons. Getting the same results time after time reduces the probability of making a decision error.

In summary, the sample size and choice of significance level will affect the probability of drawing the wrong conclusions. Usually, researchers do not know which type of error is made, but they are concerned about which type to risk making. This means that a decision should be made as to which type of error a researcher can best tolerate in a study and this in turn will determine the choice of significance level and influence the sample size. To play the game of statistical inference honestly, the decision about the significance level should really be made *before* the statistical test is carried out, when the null hypothesis is stated. Though widely practised, reporting just the most significant level found as the statistical tests are performed is not proper, since this implies that the criterion for acceptance/rejection of the null hypothesis was not set ahead of time.

There are a large number of statistical tests that will allow the comparison of pairs of groups, whole sets of groups etc. All of these tests basically share the same characteristic: a test of some null hypothesis. The same issues as identified above will apply when interpreting the results. The tests only tell whether or not the differences are statistically significant: did they occur by chance alone or was there probably some outside influence? The same questions as to which type of error, Type I or II, is to be risked must be considered. What *should* the significance level be? How small a sample can the study withstand? As you were warned, while this book treats the issues and stages in individual chapters, in reality, the necessary decisions are all interrelated and consequently will often need to be made considering several of the issues together. Now decide which errors are most likely in Activity 6.2 (p. 130).

Correlational studies

Though there are many ways of classifying research, this book uses the type of design and method of statistical analysis as the source of rubrics. For further detailed information, the reader is recommended to see such books as Cohen and Manion (1989) and Rowntree (1981) for limited mathematical treatments, Chase (1985) and Clegg (1982) for elementary

---

Activity 6.2

Below are two descriptions of research projects. For each, consider the type of error the researcher has possibly made, a Type I or a Type II (model answers are at the end of the chapter):

(a)   A researcher gave a class an IQ test and found the mean to be 108, and rejected the null hypothesis that they were not different from the population; in other words, he concluded that they were not typical of the population. Later the teacher told him that this was the third time that they had taken an IQ test in a month and were probably becoming test-wise. Which type of error has he possibly made? Why? What could be done to avoid this error?

(b)   A researcher selected 200 adults from eight randomly selected rural adult education classes on local history in his county to participate in a test of knowledge about banking. Their mean score was not significantly different from those from the whole county, thus the null hypothesis that rural adults were no less knowledgeable was accepted. Subsequently it was found that six of the adult education centres selected were in commuter areas for the main city. Which type of error has possibly been made? Why? What could be done to avoid this error?

---

mathematical introduction to statistical tests, and Blalock (1979), Dayton (1970), Ferguson (1976), Guilford and Fruchter (1973), and Winer (1971) for the most detailed mathematical approach. Three fundamental ways of analysing and presenting the results of measurement-based studies using inferential statistics are correlational, quasi-experimental and experimental studies. Correlational studies will be considered below and the other two approaches in Chapter 7.

What do correlations tell us?

Correlational studies are concerned with investigating the relationship between pairs of variables. This does *not* mean establishing cause and effect relations, since correlations only indicate the strength of relations between variables and regression equations tell how one variable changes with respect to another. For example, there is a high correlation between age and height for a range of ages of children, but neither one causes the other. In this case, growth determined by genes and nutrition are the causes. Correlations should be tested to see if they are statistically significant, to determine whether or not they occurred by chance alone, but this still has nothing to do with proving causation. Occasionally a report will state or imply causal relationships on the basis of correlations, but it requires a much more structured study to determine and begin to justify such claims, the subject of Chapter 7.

How can we visualize what is meant by correlation and regression? Data for such calculations consist of pairs of numbers for each subject, for example for a given child, what is his or her height and weight? If we plot these pairs of numbers for all of our sample, a *bivariate distribution* can be produced: two variables plotted against each other (as opposed to a frequency distribution with one variable against frequency of occurrence). This looks like numerous points on a graph, for our example, of weight versus height, which is usually referred to as a *scatter diagram*.

A high correlation (indicating a strong relationship) might come from a scatter diagram that looks like Figure 6.5A. A weak relationship and a low correlation would have a scatter diagram like Figure 6.5B. If we had *no* correlation ($r = 0.00$), it would look something like Figure 6.5C. And occasionally, the situation arises where one variable decreases as another increases, producing a negative correlation, such as shown in Figure 6.5D.

By implication from these examples, it appears that correlations are calculated for interval or ratio (continuous) variables. It is possible to

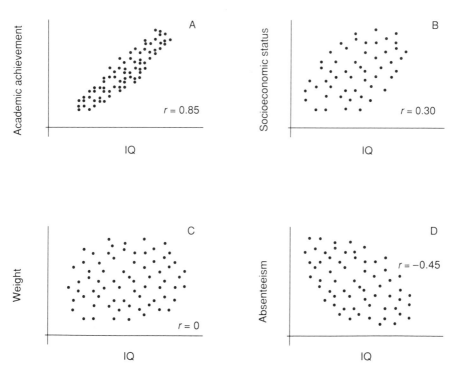

Figure 6.5 *Scatter diagrams for different correlations: A, a large positive; B, a small positive; C, no correlation; and D, a negative correlation (after Cohen and Manion, 1989).*

Table 6.1   *Some common correlation coefficients for all combinations of data pair types*

	Interval/ratio (continuous)	Ordinal	Nominal (dichotomous)
Interval/ratio (continuous)	Pearson product moment, r_{xy}	↑	Point-biserial correlation
Ordinal	←	Spearman's rho rank order correlation, ρ	Kendal's tau, τ
Nominal (dichotomous)	Point-biserial correlation	Kendal's tau, τ	Phi, φ correlation

calculate correlations for ranked (ordinal) data, for example to show the relationship between the rankings of children on learning disability by a school psychologist and a written examination. Or, to see how closely the rankings of children with learning disabilities by a classroom teacher compare with those of a visiting psychologist.

Obviously not all of these combinations involve only interval or ratio data. It is possible to find correlations between combinations of interval, ratio or ordinal data, and dichotomous (nominal) groupings. For example, it is possible to find the correlation between attitudes towards science and sex of the students (ordinal versus nominal). It is even possible to correlate two dichotomous variables, such as voter's sex and choice of two candidates (nominal versus ordinal). Details and methods of calculating appropriate coefficients, such as those in Table 6.1, are in more advanced texts.

Guilford and Fruchter (1973) suggest the following four combinations of predictions that can be made, each presented with examples:

1   *Attributes from other attributes*: predict incidence of divorce from social class, political party affiliation, or religious creed.
2   *Attributes from measurements*: predict divorce incidence from scores on a test of ability.
3   *Measurements from attributes*: predict probable test scores from sex, socioeconomic status, or marital status.
4   *Measurements from other measurements*: predict academic achievement from aptitude scores.

How are correlational relationships used? For example, given a scatter diagram of weight versus height, would it be possible to predict the weight of someone knowing their height by using such a graph of a sample of a number of people? Is it possible to predict height from weight? Figure 6.6A is just such a plot, each dot representing persons having that combination of weight and height. Taking a value of weight, such as 50 kg, there is a wide range of possible heights, ranging from 0.9m to 1.5m, some more likely than others. A more illuminating scatter diagram has how many subjects there are at each point, as in Figure 6.6B. Making a prediction becomes a little more plausible.

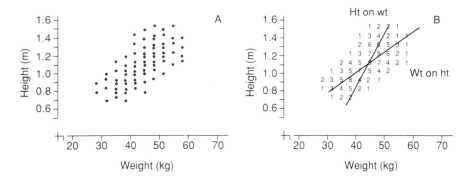

Figure 6.6   *Scatter diagrams for weight versus height for a sample of school children: A, just raw data; B, with regression lines (correlation = 0.80).*

Looking at scatter plots and trying to make predictions would be a frustrating task. As seen in Figure 6.5, even for a high correlation, there is a spread of data points. To be able to make reasonably consistent predictions (accuracy is something that will be considered later), a best-fit straight line is drawn through the data: the regression line.

Regression

Taking the process of analysis in correlational studies one step further involves calculating a *regression coefficient* (for interval/ratio data) which tells us the slope (angle with respect to the horizontal axis) of the best straight line through the scatter diagram for predicting height from weight. But because of the scatter of the points, there is actually a second possible best straight line for predicting the reverse, weight from height. These two regression lines are shown in Figure 6.6B. How these are calculated are beyond this text (see for example, Chase, 1985), but what a reader of research must consider is how these values are used. For example, trying to make 'exact' predictions from regression equations when the correlation is very low will result in very uncertain results. The correlation basically indicates the *strength* of the prediction. Thus, the lower the correlation, the greater the angle between the two regression lines. This would result in wildly different predictions. Now look at Activity 6.3 (on p. 134).

How accurate can predictions be?

Ferguson (1976) summarizes the problem of interpreting the meaning of correlation coefficients by noting that these are *not* proportions, thus 'a coefficient of 0.60 does not represent a degree of relationship twice a great as a coefficient of 0.30.' Also, he observes that the difference between 0.40 and 0.50 is not the same as the difference between 0.50 and 0.60. So what

Activity 6.3

In Figure 6.6B, find the predicted height for someone weighing 50 kg using the 'Ht on wt' line by drawing a line up from that point on the weight axis, then drawing another line to the height axis. Then take this height and predict the weight by extending your horizontal line until in intersects with the 'Wt on ht' line, then dropping a vertical line to the weight axis.

Do you get 50 kg again? How much difference is there? Would there be more or less difference if the angle between the lines were greater? Repeat the above process by starting with different weights.

does the magnitude of a correlation mean? One approach is to consider variances and the shapes of distributions, which will be done visually, keeping the mathematics of the arguments to a minimum.

A scatter diagram of a correlation of 1.00 would consist of a perfect line of dots, which would correspond to the regression line, but this rarely (if ever) exists when looking at correlations between human characteristics. As Guilford and Fruchter (1973) note, it is possible to think of a regression line as a set of mean scores with the dots on either side showing the amount of variance in the sample at a given point. If you can find variance, you can find a standard deviation, and if you can find a standard deviation, you can imagine a normal curve. Figure 6.7 shows a scatter diagram for height versus age for a large group of children between the ages of 8 and 18 years, with a high correlation, $r_{xy} = 0.90$. If one were to use this graph to predict the height of a group of 14-year-olds, it would be 1.4 metres, going

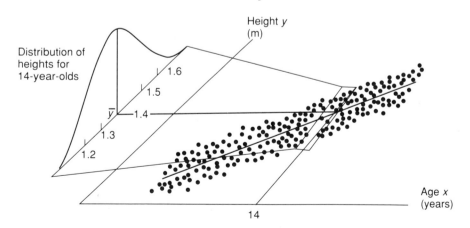

Figure 6.7   *Scatter diagram for height versus age for a group of children 8–18 years old: finding the most likely height for 14-year-olds.*

up to the regression line and over to the y-axis. Yet even the raw data draw attention to the fact that this might not be the only possible value. Remember that the researcher is making inferences about the whole population based upon this sample. There will be natural variability within the sample and there will potentially be some error due to sampling. It is best to consider the predicted value as the most likely value, but not the only possible height. The same would be true for any other prediction, be it for 13.5-year-olds, 16.7-year-olds etc., the predictions will be the most likely height. Personal experience confirms the fact that children of a given age are not all the same height.

The reverse is true as well. It is possible to predict the age of a child by looking at his or her height, but again there will be a range of possible values with a most likely one for a given population. This is illustrated in Figure 6.8 where the scatter diagram is approached from the opposite direction: taking a height of 1.4 metres, what is the most likely age? If the standard deviation of this distribution were known, then even the certainty of the prediction could be stated: 95 per cent certain that it is between ±2 standard deviations. Such data (along with other techniques) might be used by an archaeologist or forensic scientist trying to determine the age of a child from its skeleton, though knowledge of the growth rate in the population might not be very accurate, adding to uncertainty in the estimate of age at death.

The standard deviation of these distributions (which are assumed to be

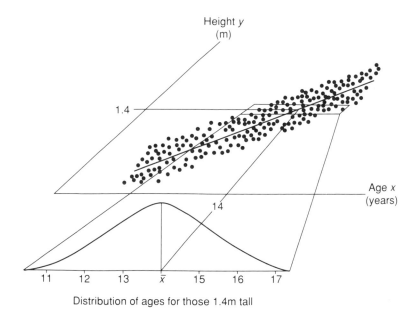

Figure 6.8 *Scatter diagram for height versus age for a group of children 8–18 years old; finding the most likely age for a child of height 1.4m.*

the same anywhere along the regression line) is called the *standard error of
the estimate*. They can be found by considering data in a given interval, say
between 13.5 and 14.5. Obviously, the smaller the correlation, the greater
the scatter of data points and the larger the standard error of the estimate.
This means that for large correlations, the 95 per cent confidence interval,
roughly ± 2 standard deviations either side of the prediction (i.e. the
interval in which there is a 95 per cent probability that the predicted value
will fall) will be small. For small correlations, the standard error of the
estimate will be larger, the 95 per cent confidence interval will be larger,
and the relative accuracy of the prediction lower.

To illustrate this slightly differently, consider another set of values, this
time scores on two tests taken by a group: an achievement test with scores
x, and an attitude measure with scores y. Since both tests produce a mean
and standard deviation, these can be used along with the correlation
between the two sets of scores to produce values for the standard error of
the estimate:

$$s_{xy} = s_x \sqrt{1 - r_{xy}^2} \qquad\qquad (3)$$

$$s_{yx} = s_y \sqrt{1 - r_{xy}^2} \qquad\qquad (4)$$

The first is for predicting attitude scores, y, from scores on the achievement
test, x, and the second for predicting achievement test scores, x, from
scores on the attitude measure, y. This shows the affect of the correlation
coefficient on the accuracy of any prediction directly: the larger r_{xy}, the
smaller the standard error of the estimate, and vice versa.

Some researchers find it useful to report the results of correlational
studies in another form. This involves explaining the variation in one
variable by variations in the other variable. This can be done by taking the
square of the correlation coefficient. For example, Figure 6.6 shows the
scatter diagram for height versus weight for a sample of school children,
which resulted in a correlation of 0.80. Thus, it is possible to say that
$(0.80)^2$ or 0.64 or 64 per cent of the variation in height is explained by the
variation in weight. This gives a different view to the meaning of strength
of correlations. If the correlation were only 0.30, then the variation in
height associated with weight would only be $(0.30)^2 = 0.09 = 9$ per cent.
Thus, according to Rowntree (1981), there is little profit in using regression
equations to predict one value from another unless the correlation is
greater than 0.80, as can be seen by calculating a series of values for
$r_{xy}^2 \times 100$, shown in Table 6.2. The remaining variance not attributable to
the other variable is assumed to be 'error', whose source is basically
anything not accounted for, including sampling errors and even other
variables.

Statistical significance

Some studies will include all correlations for all combinations of variables.
While this may seem to be a way of identifying possible relations, there is

Table 6.2 *A selection of correlation coefficients and corresponding*
impact on the proportion of variance in x *attributable to the variance in*
y, *when making predictions*

r_{xy}	% attributable $r_{xy}^2 \times 100$
0.10	1
0.20	4
0.30	9
0.40	16
0.50	25
0.60	36
0.70	49
0.80	64
0.90	81

an increased danger that statistically significant correlations will occur by chance alone. This increased risk of a Type I error would involve rejecting the null hypothesis that the correlations occurred by chance alone, when it was really true that they were a random occurrence, and thus not indicative of any relationship.

One other source of confusion arises from the use of the word 'significant'. Remember that just because a study reports a statistical significance does not necessarily mean that it has found anything of educational, sociological or psychological significance. For example, for large samples, it is possible to have statistically significant correlations (it probably did not occur by chance alone) that are numerically very small. Sear (1983) found correlations ranging from 0.17 to 0.35 between A-level grades and subsequent university degree classification, using results for (apparently) all 1979 graduates. A correlation of this size means very little in practical terms, except to other researchers looking for ideas for more research. Rowntree (1981) provides a useful classification of correlations, shown in Table 6.3.

Up to this point, it may have seemed that all relations are linear: an increase in one variable resulting in a direct increase (or decrease) in the other. Though less common, there are non-linear (curvilinear) relationships as well, such as that for the age of mothers versus number of children

Table 6.3 *Classification of strength of correlations, both positive and*
negative (after Rowntree, 1981)

Range $(+/-)$	Relative strength
0.0 to 0.2	Very weak, negligible relationship
0.2 to 0.4	Weak, low association
0.4 to 0.7	Moderate association
0.7 to 0.9	Strong, high, marked association
0.9 to 1.0	Very high, very strong relationship

born: not all age groups are equally likely to have babies, nor does the frequency necessarily increase consistently with age. Correlation and regression coefficients can be calculated for such non-linear relations as well, the details of which can be found in more advanced texts. Again, such correlations can be checked for statistical significance. Now see Activity 6.4.

Activity 6.4

(a) Sketch a scatter diagram for the suggested non-linear relationship between ages of mothers and number of children born for a sample of mothers.

(b) A report states that the correlation between teachers' assessments and examination board examination results was found to be 0.70. What might this suggest?

Factor analysis

Finally, factor analysis is a method of analysing a large number of measures to identify underlying variables (Kerlinger, 1986). Because of the rather complex nature of the calculations, it has only become popular as a research tool since the advent of computer-based statistics packages. While it is a very powerful process, it is also one that is subject to abuse. The process identifies specific 'factors' or constructs in a measuring instrument that belong together and measure virtually the same thing. For example, it has been found through this process that verbal ability, numerical ability, abstract reasoning, spatial reasoning, memory etc. all underlie intelligence (Kerlinger, 1986).

The results of a factor analysis appear as a square matrix table of correlations among potential contributing factors. For example, Kerlinger (1986) presents the correlations among the results of six (mythical) tests given to pupils, showing how common traits manifest themselves (see Table 6.4) though, as he notes, usually the clusters are not so obvious. Further manipulations and more objective tests are usually needed to highlight clusters and determine the statistical significance of the results, which would establish the soundness of contributions to a common factor(s), if they were to exist. The number is not restricted to two, and in fact most studies produce more than two clusters, but the more there are, the more difficult it is to make any sense of the results.

The main problem of use, and the primary source of abuse, originates in the choice of potential factors. This analysis is based on the assumption that each factor is a valid and reliable measure of a trait, such as the scores from a test, questionnaire or observation schedule. Because of the nature of the computer programs that carry out the calculations for factor analysis, there have been cases where individual questions on a test or

Table 6.4 *Correlational table for a mythical factor analysis on tests scores for various tests given to a group of pupils (after Kerlinger, 1986)*

	Vocab.	Reading	Syn.	Numbers	Arith. (std.)	Arith. (teach.)
Vocabulary		0.72	0.63	0.09	0.09	0.00
Reading		CLUSTER 1	0.57	0.15	0.16	0.09
Synonyms				0.14	0.15	0.09
Numbers					0.57	0.63
Arithmetic (std.)					CLUSTER 2	0.72
Arithmetic (teach.)						

questionnaire have been used. This is an extremely poor practice considering the almost total lack of reliability and validity any single question can ever have! The fact that the computer cannot tell the difference between the mean score for a number of respondents answering a single item and the mean of a set of whole test scores for a group, does not mean the program should not be used. Again, here is a case where potential abuse is not rooted in the choice of statistical test or the computer program, but in the design of the measuring instruments that are the basis of the analysis.

Criteria for evaluating inferential statistics

The following are some guidelines for applying the criteria in this column of the Profiling Sheet, with specific notes on correlational studies:

Appropriate choice of design and sound H_0. This and the next criterion are very difficult to judge. While the null hypothesis can be evaluated as to whether the correlations found were significant, often a study does not tell you enough to know whether or not the design is the best. Also, some studies could have considered the interaction of more variables, but have not done so through oversight. Sometimes the limitations are resources, which influence the sample size and therefore the complexity of the study.

A more powerful test could have been used. This criticism can be levelled at some correlational studies; based upon the research questions asked, an experimental approach would have produced more profitable results. Until you have covered Chapter 7, this may be hard to judge. Also, the type of correlation calculated may not take advantage of the level of data collected or available: ordinal or nominal data were collected when interval or ratio data would have been more appropriate, or the test does not match the data type. The possible correlations shown in Table 6.1 that use ordinal and nominal data actually increase the risk of a Type II error (not finding a significant correlation when there is one).

Missing analysis where needed. The data were collected or available (*ex post facto*), but not analysed. Correlations could have been found and hypotheses could have been tested.

Inappropriately analysed, tests performed not appropriate. This involves errors in the other direction: finding correlations using calculations intended for interval and ratio data on data that are only nominal or ordinal. Because of the nature of the statistical tests, there is a greater risk of a Type I error because of such a choice as this (finding significant differences where they do not really exist).

No justification for analysis, post hoc *data snooping.* There are those who are like young stamp collectors, they gather data but for no planned reason. Then there is the magic trip to the computing centre where some kind soul puts the data into a statistical package and miraculously, out come statistically significant correlations! Articulate researchers can cover up this approach with clever words and conclusions. Reading reports can be a bit like looking for the 'small print' in a legal document. It is necessary to understand the rules of the game to be able to spot the more subtle violations or not meeting the assumptions of a test. This level is appropriate for those who start with no research questions or hypotheses, yet produce correlations and grandiose conclusions.

Finish this chapter by doing Activity 6.5.

Activity 6.5

Obtain articles that have used correlations and inferential statistical analysis (often easily identified by the presence of probabilities, e.g. $P < 0.05$, for significance levels). Evaluate each using copies of the Profiling Sheet at the end of the chapter.

References

Blalock, H.M. (1979) *Social Statistics*, rev. 2nd edn. McGraw-Hill.

Chase, C.I. (1985) *Elementary Statistical Procedures*, 3rd edn. McGraw-Hill.

Clegg, F. (1982) *Simple Statistics: a Course Book for the Social Sciences.* Cambridge University Press.

Cohen, L. and Manion, L. (1989) *Research Methods in Education*, 3rd edn. Routledge.

Dayton, C.M. (1970) *The Design of Educational Experiments.* McGraw-Hill.

Ferguson, G.A. (1976) *Statistical Analysis in Psychology and Education*, 4th edn. McGraw-Hill.

Guilford, J.P. and Fruchter, B. (1973) *Fundamental Statistics in Psychology and Education*, 5th edn. McGraw-Hill.

Kerlinger, F.N. (1986) *Foundations of Behavioral Research*, 3rd edn. Holt, Rinehart & Winston.
Rowntree, D. (1981) *Statistics without Tears: a Primer for Non-mathematicians*. Penguin.
Sear, K. (1983) 'The correlation between A level grades and degree results in England and Wales', *Higher Education*, 12: 609–19.
Winer, B.J. (1971) *Statistical Principles in Experimental Design*, 2nd edn. McGraw-Hill.

Activity model answers

Activity 6.2

(a) Type I. The familiarity with the measuring instrument has confounded the results, thus they may not accurately reflect the group's mean IQ. Possible solution: use an earlier result, if the test is acceptable.

(b) Type II. The members of the sample groups were not necessarily typical of rural adults. Two possible solutions: either the definition of 'rural adults' needs to be clarified and maybe subdivided by occupation, or a more 'typical' county should be selected. Alternatively, the results could be extended to rural adults in that county, which may have a larger proportion of rural resident commuters than nationally.

Profiling Sheet: Evaluating Inferential Statistical Analysis (to photocopy) © Thomas R. Black 1993

Article/Report: _____

Question/hypothesis (Actions 1–3/Ch. 2)	Representativeness (Actions 4–5/Ch. 3)	Data Quality I (Action 6/Ch. 4)	Data Quality II (Action 6/Ch. 4)	Descriptive Statistics (Action 7/Ch. 5)	Inferential Statistical Analysis (Action 7/Ch. 6)
Valid question or hypothesis based on accepted theory with well-justified referenced support	Whole population	Educationally, sociologically, psychologically etc. significant and manageable number of concepts	Commercially produced and tested with high validity, reliability and objectivity (V, R, O)	Appropriate display of data and results	Appropriate choice of design, and sound H_0
Valid question or hypothesis based on own theory, well justified	Random selection from a specified population	Limited academic significance, very narrow perspective	Project produced and tested with high V, R, O	Some inadequacies, incorrectness in data/results display	A more powerful test could have been used
Credible question/hypothesis but alternatives possible, or too extensive/global, or support missing	Purposive sampling from a specified population	Large number of concepts, potentially confusing	Commercially or project produced with moderate V, R, O	Other methods of display data/results would be more appropriate	Missing analysis where needed
Weak question/hypothesis, or poorly stated, or justified with inappropriate references	Volunteers	Too many concepts and variables investigated to result in any meaning	Commercially or project produced with low V, R, O or no information provided	Serious misconceptions through use of descriptive statistics	Inappropriately analysed, tests performed not appropriate
No question or hypothesis stated, or inconsistent with known facts	Unidentified group	Trivial concepts, not academically significant	Inappropriate instrument for this application	Intentionally misleading use of descriptive statistics	No justification for analysis, *post hoc* data snooping

Comments:

7

Statistical Inference and Experimental Designs

Correlational studies allow the researcher to see if there is any relationship between pairs of variables, the correlation indicating the relative strength of the relationship. Usually there is insufficient control in such designs to allow any proof of cause and effect. To determine the possibility of existence of such a relationship the researcher must have much greater control over the possible variables that may influence any outcome, and hypothesize such a relationship before beginning the study. Again, because of the nature of the variables (frequently normally distributed around a mean that indicates the central tendency of the groups), any conclusions usually will be 'probablies'. Ultimately, much of the strength of these conclusions rests with the rigour of the design and its execution. Since most of the designs require the researcher to exercise control over variables, either directly or indirectly, these designs borrow from biological studies and are usually referred to as *experimental designs*.

Types of designs

Obviously, since they must contend with human beings as the object of their investigations, social science researchers rarely have the complete control over variables that the biologist in the laboratory does. Consequently, greater ingenuity is required of the social scientist to compensate for this lack of direct control, in order still to use the powerful statistical tests about to be considered. Therefore, the designs used in the social sciences described below have attracted names, such as *ex post facto* and quasi-experimental, that indicate this lack of absolute control usually associated with truly experimental designs. This does not detract from the potential appropriateness and power of such designs, but does indicate that there are a number of new assumptions that must be met to employ these validly, and limitations that must be recognized. Often it is the lack of rigour in designing a study or the faults in execution, rather than the use of more complex statistical tests, which ultimately weakens or totally invalidates the conclusions made in the final research report.

Experimental designs do compel the researcher to identify a limited number of potential variables, define them rigorously, propose their relationship and control all others by one means or another. Herein lies the problem: human activity is subject to a myriad of variables.

Ex post facto *studies*

Ex post facto simply means after the fact. This approach uses existing data, such as those in statistical records, or depends upon existing characteristics of the subjects, like the amount of education they have, what type of school they attend(ed), and the occupation or social class of their parents. Kerlinger (1986, ch. 22) provides a comprehensive discussion of this type of research for those interested in greater detail, although in his latest edition, he refers to this as 'nonexperimental research'. Though the goals of identifying causal relationships, the defining operationally of variables and the employment of statistical tools are often the same as used in truly experimental studies (see below), the difference lies in the degree of control the researcher has over the variables. In reality, it is not possible to have complete control over the independent variables, such as educational background, social class or genetic inheritance, since they have already occurred or cannot be manipulated.

Consider a study where the researcher wished to determine if there were any relationship between parental education and children's achievement in school. A truly experimental design to resolve issues would not be plausible since it is simply not possible to arrange for a random selection of children to be assigned to new families. An appropriate *ex post facto* study would go a long way to answering such questions, through representative sampling across families with a range of parental education, measuring and observing, and inferences based on statistical tests. But the results would always lack the maximum amount of certainty since all the possible independent variables could not be totally controlled. This is not to demean the approach, just to point up its potential limitations and the greater demand this places upon the researcher to ensure that his/her sample is representative of the population, for example here, with respect to parental education.

Much social science research that employs statistical tests is *ex post facto*, rather than truly experimental, and potentially valuable in its contribution to knowledge. It is carried out in the real world, rather than in a laboratory. The challenge for the researcher is to ensure maximum control of potential contributing factors that might constitute competing hypotheses, through appropriate choice of experimental design and sampling. Difficulty for the reader of research reports arises because both *ex post facto* and experimental designs will employ the same statistical tests (like analysis of variance). In such situations, the designs are sometimes referred to as quasi-experimental. The main interest then is to determine whether or not sampling has been appropriate and variables have been controlled. The reader may have to infer the use of an *ex post facto* design if this has not been stated outright.

The choice of design and availability of data will also affect what questions can actually be answered. If measures of the desired variables do not exist or were not collected reliably (such as statistical records not being kept, data not collected properly, samples not being representative), then some questions cannot be answered after the fact. For example, to resolve the issue of whether people are taller today than in past years would require representative data (emphasis on representative) from the past as well as the present. Looking for possible sources going back over time, the question arises, do available military records supply valid data? The answer is, only if it could be proved that conscripts and volunteers constituted a representative cross-section of society. Recognizing that throughout history there has been a tendency for many men to avoid being conscripted, this may not be true. One could argue that those who escaped military service in the past were the better educated and consequently better fed, and would not be proportionally represented among those serving. Thus the overall physical attributes (means and standard deviations) of conscripts and volunteers may not be representative of the whole population at that time. The researcher would have to establish the representativeness of the data through (historical) research. This is indicative of the type of questions that would have to be considered if existing data were to be used for an *ex post facto* study.

Experimental studies

These differ from other types of research in that there is the possibility of manipulation and control of the hypothesized independent variable (the treatment) by the researcher. Also, there tends to be the requirement that subjects should be randomly assigned to treatment groups so as to eliminate the influence of mediating and extraneous variables. Though this approach has the potential of providing more meaningful data, it tends to be costly and not always possible, as seen earlier with the impossibility of assigning children to new families. Also, there has been the criticism made that experimental research in education often lacks realism, relevance to classroom problems and rigour (Lehmann and Mehrens, 1979). These studies have frequently been conducted to compare the effectiveness of different teaching and learning methods, using available groups, and the effects of various variables on memory, using undergraduate psychology student volunteers. The last point is simply a reflection of the general difficulty of carrying out research involving human beings and controlling all the possible variables in their lives. This tendency towards the use of convenience samples has provided a negative contribution to the debate on appropriate use of such designs. This just emphasizes the problem that, as with all other types of research, the skills and care needed to carry out such studies properly are numerous and the pitfalls many.

Keeping these potential problems in mind, both approaches, experimental and quasi-experimental, employ common designs and statistics. What differentiates the designs is how many variables will be considered in a given study, which usually means how many different groups of subjects (each differing on one or more variables) will be used.

Number of groups

Using inferential statistics to determine the acceptability of hypotheses requires an understanding of the limitations of this tool. Statistically based designs have a variety of different tests from which to choose, the choice depending on how many groups are involved. Basically the possible questions that can be answered are whether:

- one sample group belongs to a well-defined population;
- two unrelated groups belong to the same population (not necessarily well defined);
- two related groups belong to the same population; or
- three or more groups belong to the same population for some given trait.

The actual design of the study and how the hypothesis is phrased will be related to how many groups are involved. This will provide a convenient way of viewing different types of design that employ statistical tests.

One-sample group

In Chapter 6, the case of a single group was used as the example when explaining statistical inference. The question was asked, with respect to IQ, does this sample of 40 children appear to belong to the population of all 11-year-olds? In other words, even though the mean IQ test score for the sample (in this case, 106) is not the same as the population mean of 100, is it close enough to the population mean for the group to be considered part of the population, or is it so far away that the sample group should be thought part of another population? In other words, is it considered an example of the natural variation in IQ test scores or not? This example used interval data, but the question can also be asked and answered for situations which lead to an operational definition of the trait that results in the collection of ordinal or nominal data, as will be seen later.

Two independent groups

This class of tests involves comparing two groups on some trait and asking: do these two unrelated groups belong to the same population? For this type of test, knowledge of the population is not necessary as the statistics of the two groups are used as a basis for the decision. Basically, if the test decides that the two probably do not belong to the same population, there is no indication as to what populations they do belong. The question is a simple one: do the two groups belong to the same population, whatever that may be? Often, the questions that are resolved by such tests are stated in terms of causal relationships between variables: whatever is being measured (like height, income, IQ) being the *dependent variable* because the scores are hypothesized to depend upon the groups to which subjects belong, the *independent variable* (such as social class, treatment group, age range). Unfortunately, when hypotheses are stated this way, the implication is that if a significant difference is found, a causal relationship exists. As noted time and time again, this is *not* necessarily so. If one has a truly experimental design, then there is a much better chance of proving this than if the design is quasi-experimental or *ex post facto*, where control over variables is more tenuous. The proof, though, is separate from the statistical test and dependent on adequate control of variables.

There has been an enormously wide variety of applications of tests between two independent groups. Campbell and Stanley (1963) note that the main sources of faults to look for when such a design is employed are:

(a) how the groups are formed or members selected, and
(b) whether or not the membership stays constant throughout the experiment or experience.

For example, to answer the perennial question of which are 'better', private schools or state schools, one could compare examination results for representative samples of each. This could be done in Britain by considering GCSE (General Certificate of Secondary Education) examination results or in America by using the SAT (Scholastic Aptitude Test) results. First, the two general issues identified above must be addressed as specific questions: (a) were the groups equivalent in the first place, thus were both groups representative of the whole population of children at entry age for all traits that might affect examination success? And (b) did all those that started in each group finish? If one looks at the children in both types of schools, there tend to be some rather extreme differences for a variety of variables: social class, parental income and race. For criteria (b), most (though not all) in both groups last until the examinations are taken, though the drop-out rate tends to be higher in state schools. So while the question could be asked, data collected and a statistical test used to answer the question, using raw examination results is hardly a valid approach.

Consider a second, but less ambitious, study: it would be possible to compare two teaching approaches, if the conditions described above were satisfied by (a) randomly allocating learners to the two groups, and (b) ensuring that there were no 'drop-outs'. The problem with this type of study (commonly reported in the literature) is finding truly representative groups: as noted earlier, too often available groups are used.

Returning to the first research question, it is impossible to assign pupils randomly to state or private schools, thus it would be impossible to eliminate totally the problem of non-equivalent groups. The degree of equivalence in the samples would be determined by sampling techniques.

The second issue could be addressed by using gain scores (measure them when they enter and measure them when they leave), then it matters less who stays or leaves, thus satisfying condition (b). This would require a more explicit definition of 'better' when referring to the relative effectiveness of schools.

The second exemplar research question on teaching approaches raises different problems. For many designs where the question of testing the effectiveness of learning materials or strategies is to be resolved, randomly allocating learners to the two groups and providing pre- and post-tests ensures that most competing hypotheses are eliminated (Campbell and Stanley, 1963). Here the problem has been proving that the original group that was divided in two was truly representative of the whole population of learners. Usually they are not, since they are students who are available to the researcher at the time, therefore weakening any case made. This does not necessarily totally invalidate such studies, but the reader should be aware of the affect this has on the strength of any inferences extended to a larger population.

Similar criticisms have been levelled at studies in other areas. Numerous psychological studies have been conducted using undergraduate volunteers. Sociological investigations have drawn on coherent groups like workers in a specific car assembly factory, a local coal mining community, a suburb of a city or farmers in one locality.

Two related groups

This type of test involves two groups that are related in some way and asking whether or not they belong to the same population. For example, at the simplest level, a researcher might want to know if a teaching approach were effective by applying a pre- and post-test to his/her class and testing for a significant difference. Since the same students would be doing both tests, they would constitute related groups. Unfortunately, there are several competing hypotheses even if a significant difference were found. For example, something else may have enhanced learning, the learners matured, they became test-wise etc. Using score gains and two groups (one using a traditional approach and the other the new approach) as described in the previous section (b) on unrelated groups, can eliminate the possibility of competing hypotheses providing better explanations.

The idea of related groups can contribute to an improved design if applied differently. Consider the situation where two teaching methods are to be compared, but for a fair test to be made, the two groups used should be alike and matched on such traits as intelligence, age, social class. The design would wish to determine if a change has occurred in a group, applying a test, a 'treatment' and a re-test as above. Comparing the test with the re-test involves investigating related traits since the groups have been matched according to traits that might provide competing hypotheses if ignored (Chase, 1985). Other possibilities where groups might be related for potentially confounding traits are if one wanted to compare attitudes, for example towards ethnic minorities, across generations using members of common families. As in the first case, the data gathered from each group will be influenced somewhat by the other. Using related groups can essentially control variables and consequently eliminate competing hypotheses, if used appropriately.

Three or more groups

The fourth type of statistical test involves comparing three or more groups, sometimes using complex classification schemes; for example, to determine whether or not the children in three different education authorities achieved comparable results on their examinations through gains in scores over a number of years. The measures from a sample from each could be compared to see if they all belong to the same population, which means asking: is there a significant difference across schools or sex (see Table 7.1)? What sort of data will appear in the cells or boxes will be discussed in the following sections. While this is quite straightforward, the challenge for the researcher comes in *proving* which variable(s) (if any of those identified) actually caused the difference: the efforts of the education authority, or was it ethnic origin of the students, quality of the individual schools, support by groups of parents, student anxiety, water supply, air pollution, number and/or quality of books in local public library etc.? Some of the variables chosen for such studies are so ill defined as to be meaningless, such as social class (ask six different sociologists to classify a group of, say, 50 people into different classes: how many and what constitutes membership are often quite contentious) or anxiety (imagine what sort of agreement there would be among six psychologists when confronted with the task of placing each of 50 people into one of five levels of anxiousness). This is complicated by the fact that rarely is something so complex as examination results influenced primarily by one variable.

Thus the main problem for the reader is not so much in the design, but the variables chosen. These four basic designs and the resulting statistical tests to be discussed below will only tell whether there is a difference, not what caused it, thus the real skill comes in selecting a *meaningful* question and identifying educationally, sociologically or psychologically significant variables when first designing the investigation, followed by the use of

Table 7.1 A quasi-experimental design to determine whether there is any difference in the examination results across local education authorities (LEAs) (not necessarily a good study)

	Frogfield LEA	Turnip Green LEA	North Noodle LEA
Boys			
Girls			

reliable and valid measuring instruments, as noted in earlier chapters. Almost anyone can put numbers into a computer program and find statistical significance, but it takes a very well-planned study to ask a significant question, and find a meaningful answer using the statistical results. You should now carry out Activity 7.1.

Activity 7.1

1　Classify the examples of designs in the above four sections as either (a) *ex post facto* quasi-experimental, or (b) experimental, and be able to defend your choice.
2　Consider the following research question and suggested design: Do girls perform better in mixed or single-sex schools? Ten schools of each type were randomly selected across the country and standardized examination results for the girls were compared (two unrelated groups).
　　What are alternative hypotheses for the expected outcomes? Suggest an improved design that would either include or control these.

The following two sections will describe the types of statistical tests that can be applied, depending on what type of data (nominal, ordinal, interval or ratio) have been collected. These will be presented with minimal mathematics and you are encouraged to consult other texts such as those listed at the end of this chapter for more detailed treatment.

Parametric tests

When employing statistics (data collected from representative samples) to use as estimates of parameters (population data) and draw conclusions that extend to the population(s), the tests that are employed are known as *parametric tests*. To use this class of tests requires that several basic assumptions be met:

1　At least one variable will have to be interval or ratio data (most commonly this is the dependent variable).
2　The data must be normally distributed around a mean.
3　If there is more than one group, there must be homogeneity of variance, which means that all the distributions involved should have the same shape and thus roughly the same standard deviation.

If the data do not meet these criteria, then a researcher should probably be using non-parametric tests (discussed in the next section), but there are grey areas. For example, just how skewed can a distribution be before it is considered to be not normal? A visual check is the first clue, but rarely do journal articles contain histograms of raw data. It is possible to calculate a coefficient for the relative skewness of a curve (Blalock, 1979), but how much skewness is allowed is not definitive. More important is the test for homogeneity of variance, of which there are several (see Chase, 1985; Dayton, 1970; Winer, 1971). If one lacks homogeneity of variance, it is possible to 'normalize' the data, mathematically massage the numbers to force all the distributions to be much the same, though this will make it harder to find statistical significance in subsequent tests. Again, it will depend to a certain extent on the relative importance of decisions to be made on the results as to how far a researcher can deviate from the three rules above. It is not unreasonable to expect researchers at least to address these issues in a report.

Four classes of statistical test will be considered, using the four group sizes and types described above.

One-sample test

First, we have already seen in Chapter 6 how to test to see if a sample should be considered as part of a population, using z-scores, the *one-sample case*. This is a reasonable test if the population values (parameters) for the mean and standard deviation are known. Often, this is not the situation, requiring the researcher to use an estimate of the standard deviation from sample data to determine the standard error of the sampling means, $s_{\bar{x}}$. The test requires us to compare ratios, providing a t-test, which looks very similar to the z-test used earlier, to determine how many standard deviations the sample mean is from the population mean,

$$t = \frac{\bar{x}_a - \mu}{s_{\bar{x}}} \tag{1}$$

where

$\bar{x}_a$ = sample mean
μ = population mean
$s_{\bar{x}}$ = estimate of the standard error of the sampling mean found by

$$s_{\bar{x}} = \frac{s_a}{\sqrt{n_a}}$$

where

s_a = sample standard deviation
n_a = sample size

One then looks at a table such as Table 5.5 in Chapter 5 to check the likelihood of the sample belonging to the population, the same as for a z-test unless the sample is fewer than 30. Small samples do not necessarily produce the same nicely normal distribution of sample means, thus a new table of values with 5 per cent, 1 per cent etc. significance levels for each sample size, called a *t*-distribution, is used that compensates for a small sample (anything smaller than 30). The test is said to become more conservative the smaller the sample, since it then becomes more difficult to find statistical significance as the differences in the means have to be larger. Thus while the cut-off for 5 per cent significance from the original was 1.96 standard deviations, if the sample were only 20, then the *t*-ratio would have to be 2.080, and if the sample were only 10, then the *t*-ratio would have to be 2.228 for the sample to be considered significantly different. In other words, for small samples ($n < 30$), it becomes harder to find a significant difference and reject the null hypothesis. Most statistics texts have a *t*-distribution for various levels of significance in their appendices.

The reason for going into such detail at this point is to illustrate the fact that all subsequent tests of significance have tables that depend upon sample size. So even though the tests change, they all include a compensation to take into account sample size, making it harder to find significance for smaller samples.

Two independent groups

This class of test involves comparing two groups on some trait and asking: do these two groups belong to the same population? If the data are interval or ratio, the question is answered by comparing the means and using the two standard deviations to generate an estimate of the standard error of the mean now called the *standard error of the difference*, s_{diff}, as follows,

$$t = \frac{\bar{x}_a - \bar{x}_b}{s_{\text{diff}}} \tag{2}$$

where

$\bar{x}_a$ = mean of first sample
$\bar{x}_b$ = mean of second sample
s_{diff} = estimate of the standard error of the difference found
            by

$$s_{\text{diff}} = \sqrt{s_a^2 + s_b^2}$$

where

s_a = standard deviation of first sample
s_b = standard deviation of second sample

Typically, a report will provide results in a form similar to those shown in Table 7.2. This simply provides the means, standard deviations and sample sizes of the two groups, plus the value for the *t*-statistic and its probability level (if it is significant). Again, the level of significance is dependent upon the sample size (n) so a *t*-distribution is used. Note that most often no graphs or charts will be provided and the reader will be expected to

Table 7.2 *Statistics calculated for testing the difference between two independent samples (H_0 is rejected)*

	Group A	Group B
$\bar{x}$	21.0	18.0
s	4.0	5.0
n	22	25
$t = 2.28, p < 0.05$		

visualize the distributions based upon the means, $\bar{x}_a$ and $\bar{x}_b$, and standard deviations, s_a and s_b, presented.

Two related groups

This type of test involves two groups that are related in some way, as described earlier. For example, as noted above, it could involve a situation where two teaching methods are to be compared, but for a fair test to be made the two groups used should be alike on such traits as intelligence. We may wish to determine if a change has occurred in a group, applying a test, a 'treatment' and a re-test. Comparing the test to the re-test involves investigating related traits. To test for significance in such situations is the same as for two unrelated groups, except that the calculation of the standard error of the difference is slightly different,

$$s_{\text{diff}} = \sqrt{s_a^2 + s_b^2 - 2r_{ab}s_a s_b}$$

where

s_a = standard deviation of first sample
s_b = standard deviation of second sample
r_{ab} = the correlation between the two groups

The reader would be presented with a table similar to Table 7.2 again, though the relationship between the groups would be mentioned in the text of the report since the underlying calculations would be different.

There are actually two possible ways of reporting significance for two groups. If the researcher has not anticipated which way the difference between the means of the groups would be, then it could be that $\bar{x}_a > \bar{x}_b$ or that $\bar{x}_b > \bar{x}_a$, and it is assumed that it could go either way, therefore a *two-tailed test* is applied. This means that the difference has to be sufficiently large that the *t*-score would be in either tail as in Figure 6.3. But if the researcher predicts that the difference could only be one way, for example $\bar{x}_b$ could only be greater than $\bar{x}_a$, then a *one-tailed test* would be applied, where all 5 per cent appears in one end of the distribution, as shown in Figure 7.1 for a *z*-score. Obviously it is easier to find significance for a one-tailed test since the 5 per cent level is the same as the 10 per cent level for a two-tailed test. Again, which test will be used should have been decided before the test was carried out, and the same problems of risks of Type I and Type II tests apply as noted earlier.

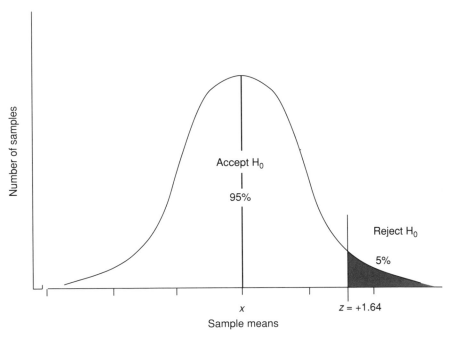

Figure 7.1   *Normal distribution of sample means with 5 per cent significance level for a one-tailed test.*

Three or more groups

The fourth group of statistical tests involves comparing three or more groups, sometimes using complex classification schemes. The test requires the simultaneous comparison of a number of groups and the parametric test that has been developed is the *analysis of variance,* or *ANOVA.* This again uses both the means and standard deviations, with all the above assumptions of normal distribution, homogeneity of variance etc. to make such comparisons, based this time on ratios of variances. Consider, for example a simpler design than the one outlined above and portrayed in Table 7.1: in this study, the intent was to compare the effectiveness of three approaches to learning. The sample was a stratified random sampling of six classes of 11–13 students each from across a local education authority

Table 7.3   *A quasi-experimental design to determine whether there is any difference in the performance across the groups learning by different approaches, using indicated gain scores as the dependent variable*

	Approach A	Approach B	Approach C	Overall
Mean, $\bar{x}$	12.50	13.60	14.00	13.38
Standard deviation, s	0.50	0.49	0.51	
Sample size, n	12	11	13	36

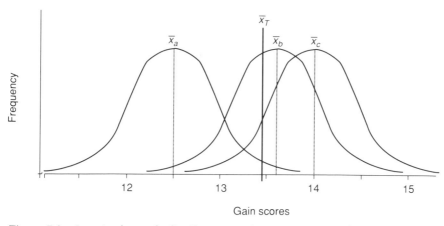

Figure 7.2 *Imagined sample distributions with group means and grand mean, $\bar{x}_T$, for the three approaches in Table 7.3.*

or school district. The results were in the form of gain scores (pre- and post-tests were administered) and the results are summarized in Table 7.3 as means and standard deviations.

From this type of results table, the reader must usually try to imagine the distributions, but these are shown in Figure 7.2 for this example. In this case, the F-test, or F-statistic, is used to determine ultimately whether or not groups experiencing the different learning approaches still belong to the same population, based upon how much of an overlap there is among all the distributions. Those in Figure 7.2 would appear to represent a significant difference across the three groups. Usually, the reader is only provided with a results table such as shown in Table 7.4., which is not very informative on its own.

The calculation of the F-statistic is presented to show how this takes into account the relationships between the three (in this case) 'treatments'. The F-statistic is calculated simply by finding the ratios of two estimates of the variance for the overall population, one based on the means of the three (in this case) groups and is based upon the individual group variances, sometimes called the error variance. The estimate of the variance for the

Table 7.4 *Statistics calculated for testing the H_0 that there was no difference across the three learning approaches, using the F-test for a one-way analysis of variance (Table 7.3 and Figure 7.2)*

	d.f.	MS	F	
Approaches (treatments)	2	7.41	29.56	$p < 0.05$
Error	45	0.25		

whole population based upon the means is called the *mean of squares for treatments* (or sometimes, among groups). The estimate of the error variance (or in some books it is called within groups variance) based upon the group variances is called the *mean of squares for error*. The calculations can be performed as follows,

$$F = \frac{MS_{\text{treat}}}{MS_{\text{error}}}$$

(3)

where

MS_{treat} = mean square treatment, or among groups, found for this situation of three groups, by,

$$MS_{\text{treat}} = \frac{n_a(\bar{x}_a - \bar{x}_T)^2 + n_b(\bar{x}_b - \bar{x}_T)^2 + n_c(\bar{x}_c - \bar{x}_T)^2}{3 - 1}$$

where

n_a, n_b, n_c = the group sample sizes
$\bar{x}_a, \bar{x}_b, \bar{x}_c$ = the group means
$\bar{x}_T$ = the grand mean of all the groups together

and

MS_{error} = means square error, or within groups, found for this situation of three groups, by,

$$MS_{\text{error}} = \frac{(n_a - 1)s_a^2 + (n_b - 1)s_b^2 + (n_c - 1)s_c^2}{n_a + n_b + n_c - 3}$$

where

s_a^2, s_b^2, s_c^2 = the group variances, standard deviations squared

The d.f. column indicates degrees of freedom, a concept related to sources of variation in measurements, described in detail in more advanced texts (e.g. Chase, 1985; Winer, 1971). As you will note, these are numerically equivalent to the denominators of the respective calculations for mean squares. The *F*-statistic is then compared to the appropriate table to see if it exceeds the value necessary for significance, and reported as in Table 7.4.

The *F*-statistic is the basis for deciding whether or not all the groups belong to the same population, and it is a way of mathematically finding what might be determined by considering the overlap of the three graphs in Figure 7.2. In this case, when the *F*-statistic was compared to a standard *F*-distribution table, it was found that the probability that all three belonged to the same group was less than 5 per cent, and thus stated as $p < 0.05$ (probability less than 0.05 in 1). This basically means that the differences in gain scores across the three learning approaches could not be attributable to chance alone. The researcher would need to provide some

Table 7.5 *Scheffé's* post hoc *test carried out across pairs of approaches to test significance differences*

	Approaches A and B	Approaches A and C	Approaches B and C	Minimum for $p < 0.05$
Scheffé statistic	5.26	7.48	1.95	2.56

justification that the only possible learning events that occurred for these groups that could have affected the scores were the experiences that they had during the classes employing the approaches. This would be needed to enhance the strength of any inference about learning approaches that would be made.

Post hoc *analysis*

For analysis of variance, one further set of tests can be performed if significance is found. The *F*-test would confirm that the three groups did not belong to a common population, but would *not* tell whether any combination of pairs belonged or did not belong to a common population. A *post hoc* analysis would allow the researcher to determine whether or not pairs of groups were significantly different. There are a number of these tests, all of which are more conservative that using multiple *t*-tests (in other words it will be more difficult to find statistical significance among pairs). These include tests in order of increasing conservatism: Duncan, Neumann–Keuls and Tukey (all for equal sample sizes), and Scheffé (which copes with unequal cell size). Each test requires the calculation of a statistic that is in turn compared to its own table of probabilities. In fact, the use of multiple *t*-tests is highly regarded as inappropriate and likely to enhance the commitment of a Type I error.

For the case above, having found a significant difference across the three approaches, the question remains whether or not those experiencing Approach A are significantly different from B or C, and whether those experiencing Approach B are significantly different from C: three combinations, A–B, A–C, and B–C. Looking at Figure 7.2, one might expect the difference between Approaches A and C to be significant and between Approaches B and C not to be, but uncertain about the difference between Approaches A and B. In fact, if the Scheffé test (Chase, 1985) is applied, it is found that Approaches A and B are significantly different and Approaches A and C are significantly different, but Approaches B and C are not, as shown in Table 7.5.

Non-parametric tests

Non-parametric tests do not have all the constraints of parametric tests: there are no assumptions about normal distributions for interval/ratio data, they are easier to use and apply, and rank and ordinal data can be analysed. They do have some requirements of their own and their disadvantage is that their use is more likely to incur a Type II error than a parallel parametric test. They are often rated against comparable parametric tests in terms of *power-efficiency*, which Siegel and Castellan (1988) describe for a test that has a power-efficiency of 90 per cent as 'when all the conditions of the parametric statistical test are satisfied the appropriate parametric test would be just as effective with a sample which is 10 per cent smaller than that used in the non-parametric analysis'.

The number and variety of tests are considerable and beyond the scope of this book (see Siegel and Castellan, 1988 for comprehensive coverage), but one of the more common ones will be used in an example to illustrate the basic differences with parametric tests: *chi-square* or χ^2.

One-sample test

As seen earlier, the question to be answered by such tests is whether or not the sample is typical or representative of a larger group. Non-parametric tests are appropriate for situations where the data are not interval or ratio. Therefore, instead of measuring a characteristic of a group and filling a frequency table with frequencies for different intervals, the frequencies are for nominal or ordinal characteristics.

Take the (fictitious) case of a survey carried out in an English village pub one evening to ascertain the political affiliation of the patrons. The question is, are they, the sample, a typical cross-section of voters in that ward, the population? The first column of numbers in Table 7.6 provides the results of the survey. Note that the patrons are grouped not according to a measurement on an interval scale (height, IQ etc.), but according to a nominal scale: political affiliation. There is no mean nor standard deviation, these have no meaning here. To resolve the question, there is a need to compare these results with the characteristics of the larger population. It was decided that the recent village council election would provided a valid indication of the voting tendencies of the ward, thus the results of the last

Table 7.6   *Chi-square test of political affiliations of patrons of the Green Toad pub on a given night, using expected affiliations based upon recent voting patterns in the ward*

Parties	Observed frequency (f_0)	Recent election (%)	Expected frequency (f_e)	$\dfrac{(f_0 - f_e)^2}{f_e}$
Labour	24	32	27.84	0.53
Conservative	18	30	26.10	2.51
Liberal Democrat	33	32	27.84	0.96
Raving Loony	12	6	5.22	8.81
Total	87	100	87.00	$\chi^2 = 12.81$
				$p < 0.05$

election appear in the second column of numbers as percentages. Using the total number of persons in the pub survey, the third column shows the expected frequencies based upon the percentages in the recent council election. The fourth column of numbers is the difference between the observed and expected frequencies squared divided by the expected frequency, to give an indication of the relative size of the variation from the expected. These are all added together to form the chi-square statistic, and again, this is checked against a probability table.

The results in Table 7.9 show that the null hypothesis, no difference between the political affiliations of those in the pub and the ward as a whole, was rejected and that the group in the Green Toad on that night would not be considered representative of the recent voting population. For those of you who are not familiar with British politics: yes, there is a Raving Loony Party, though its membership is rather small.

Two groups

As can be seen from Table 7.9 there are several possible non-parametric tests for two groups. The following example only covers one, again using the chi-square test for simplicity, to illustrate the use of such tests.

Carrying the above example a little further: in an effort to resolve whether the patrons of the Green Toad and the nearby Red Herring pub had much the same political preferences, since they were in the same ward, the patrons of the Red Herring were interviewed as well. (Consider the sampling and data collection problems: they would not be trivial!) The question here is: can they be considered to be from the same population with respect to political preference? Here, there is no comparison to the rest of the ward, but rather a comparison with each other. They could have comparable voting preferences and still both be atypical for the ward. The results for both pubs are listed in Table 7.7, called a contingency table.

To used the chi-square test in this situation, the expected frequencies column is generated from the percentages derived from combined frequencies of both surveys. These in turn are used to determine the expected frequencies, as listed in Table 7.8. The same calculation is carried out, this

Table 7.7   *Contingency table (2 × 4) showing the results of the surveys on political preference at the Green Toad and Red Herring pubs*

	Green Toad	Red Herring	Total	%
Labour	24	16	40	24.5
Conservative	18	10	28	17.2
Liberal Democrat	33	36	69	42.3
Raving Loony	12	14	26	16.0
Total	87	76	163	100.0

Table 7.8 *Chi-square test comparing political affiliations of patrons of the Green Toad and Red Herring pubs on a given night, using expected affiliations based upon combined patterns*

Parties	Observed frequency (f_0)	Expected percentage	Expected frequency (f_e)	$\dfrac{(f_0 - f_e)^2}{f_e}$
Green Toad:				
Labour	24	24.5	21.35	0.33
Conservative	18	17.2	14.94	0.62
Liberal Democrat	33	42.3	36.83	0.40
Raving Loony	12	16.0	13.88	0.25
Red Herring:				
Labour	16	24.5	18.65	0.38
Conservative	10	17.2	13.06	0.71
Liberal Democrat	36	42.3	32.17	0.46
Raving Loony	14	16.0	12.12	0.29
Total	163		163.00	$\chi^2 = 3.44$ n.s.

time for eight groups, to see if the sum produces a significant chi-square statistic, which it does not. What does this tell us? Though there is a difference, it is not significant and it could be attributed to chance alone.

Summary

Table 7.9 lists non-parametric tests comparable to the parametric ones described above, including tests for three or more groups. The tests that use ordinal and nominal variables for correlations shown in Table 7.9 are also non-parametric tests. In the final analysis, though, the results are interpreted in much the same way as for parametric tests.

Choosing an appropriate test is often a matter of matching the test to the type of data and, for parametric tests, making sure that all of the assumptions have been met. There is the danger of degradation of data by using a 'lower' test by considering interval data as rank-ordered data and using a non-parametric test. This can increase the risk of making a Type II error, not finding significance when it really is there. It is also possible to degrade data by considering ranked data as nominal when selecting a less appropriate test. On the other hand, sometimes the reverse happens where a parametric test is used with ranked data, particularly when total scores on questionnaires are used, a choice that can be argued when the range of scores is large. Justification for deviating from what might be expected, going either way, should be presented by researchers in their reports.

Much more complex designs than those used as examples above appear in the literature, employing multidimensional schemes, examining the potential interrelationships among an even larger number of variables. The statistical tests exist, but the interpretation becomes increasingly complex.

Table 7.9 Some typical parametric and non-parametric tests for various data type combinations and research designs

	Parametric		Non-parametric	
	Nominal groups v. interval/ratio data (normal distrib.)	Nominal groups v. continuous data (not normal distrib.)	Nominal groups v. ordinal data	Nominal groups v. nominal data
Group part of a population?	z-test t-test		Kolmogorov–Smirnov 1-sample test	1-group × n-traits χ^2
Compare two independent groups	t-test	Permutation test for 2 indep. samples	Median test Wilcoxon–Mann–Whitney test Robust rank-order test Kolmogorov–Smirnov 2-sample test	2-groups × n-traits, χ^2 2-groups × 2-trait & n≤20, Fisher exact
Compare two correlated groups	t-test (correlated groups)	Permutation test for paired replicates	Sign test Wilcoxon signed ranks test	McNemar change test (before/after)
Compare across several groups	ANOVA, F-test ANCOVA, F-test		Freidman 2-way ANOVA by ranks Kruskal–Wallis 1-way ANOVA by ranks	Cochran Q test
Post hoc (among groups) analysis	Scheffé, Tukey, Neumann–Keuls, etc.			χ^2 test r × k

Yet this is to be expected, since rarely do we find that any one human characteristic, trait or event has a single cause. As noted before, the task that faces the social science researcher is complex simply due to the nature of his or her subject, so it is not surprising that the tools are not simple either. Like any complex tool, measurement and statistics applied to complex designs require care and skill if they are to be employed appropriately. All too often, though, it is not the choice of statistical test that is at fault, but any one of the other criteria that are being considered in this book.

Criteria for evaluating inferential statistics

The following are some guidelines for applying the criteria in this column of the Profiling Sheet:

Appropriate choice of design, and sound H_0. This and the next criterion are very difficult to judge. While the null hypothesis can be evaluated, often a study does not tell you enough to know whether or not the design (experimental or quasi-experimental) is the best. Also, some studies could have considered the interaction of more variables, but have not done so through oversight, or insufficiently large sample to fill all the cells in the design. Sometimes the limitations are resources, which influence the sample size and therefore the complexity of the study.

A more powerful test could have been used. This criticism can be levelled sometimes when non-parametric tests have been employed: had the variables been measured using interval or ratio scales a more powerful parametric test could have been used. Alternatively, the test does not take advantage of the level of data (interval or ratio) that was collected and a non-parametric test has been used where a parametric one was appropriate, thus increasing the risk of a Type II error (not finding a significant difference when there was one). Tables 6.1 and 7.9 can be used as a first reference for making such decisions, though if there is still doubt, ask someone who has more experience with statistics.

Missing analysis where needed. The data were collected or available (e.g. *ex post facto*), but not analysed. Hypotheses could have been tested.

Inappropriately analysed, tests performed not appropriate. This ranges from using repeated tests on pairs (multiple *t*-tests) where a more complex design would have been appropriate, to using a parametric test on data (nominal or ordinal, or non-normally distributed data) when a non-parametric test would have been more appropriate. Because of the nature of the statistical tests, there is often a greater risk of a Type I error because of this (finding significant differences where they do not really exist).

No justification for analysis, post hoc *data snooping.* It is relatively easy to carry out multiple tests on sets of numbers and eventually find significant differences when using computer-based statistical packages. It takes little time or effort and if enough combinations are tried, something usually comes out 'significant'. Unfortunately, this approach is not justifiable and frequently produces statistical results that make no contribution to answering a research question. Some researchers will leave out the meaningless ones and report the few that seem to support their hypotheses, but selectively using results in this way is not a valid use of statistical tests. Detecting such practices is not easy, but omitted combinations are often an indication.

You should carry out Activity 7.2 now.

Activity 7.2

Obtain articles that have used inferential statistical analysis (often easily identified by the presence of probabilities, e.g. $p < 0.05$, for significance levels). Evaluate each using copies of the profile on the Profiling Sheet at the end of the chapter.

References

Blalock, H.M. (1979) *Social Statistics*, rev. 2nd edn. McGraw-Hill.

Bynner, J. and Stribley, K.M. (eds) (1978) *Social Research: Principles and Procedures*. Longman.

Campbell, D.T. and Stanley, J.C. (1963) *Experimental and Quasi-experimental Designs for Research*. Rand McNally.

Chase, C.I. (1985) *Elementary Statistical Procedures,* 3rd edn. McGraw-Hill.

Clegg, F. (1982) *Simple Statistics: a Course Book for the Social Sciences*. Cambridge University Press.

Cohen, L. and Manion, L. (1989) *Research Methods in Education,* 3rd edn. Routledge.

Dayton, C.M. (1970) *The Design of Educational Experiments*. McGraw-Hill.

Ferguson, G.A. (1976) *Statistical Analysis in Psychology and Education*, 4th edn. McGraw-Hill.

Guilford, J.P. and Fruchter, B. (1973) *Fundamental Statistics in Psychology and Education*, 5th edn. McGraw-Hill.

Kerlinger, F.N. (1986) *Foundations of Behavioral Research*, 3rd edn. Holt, Rinehart & Winston.

Lehmann, I.J. and Mehrens, W.A. (1979) *Educational Research: Readings in Focus,* 2nd edn. Holt, Rinehart & Winston.

Open University (1973) *Methods of Educational Enquiry, E341. Block 2: Research Design*. Open University Press.

Rowntree, D. (1981) *Statistics without Tears: a Primer for Non-mathematicians*. Penguin.

Sear, K. (1983) 'The correlation between A level grades and degree results in England and Wales', *Higher Education*, 12: 609–19.

Siegel, S. and Castellan, N.J. Jr (1988) *Non-parametric Statistics*, 2nd edn. McGraw-Hill.

Winer, B.J. (1971) *Statistical Principles in Experimental Design*, 2nd edn. McGraw-Hill.

Profiling Sheet: Evaluating Inferential Statistical Analysis (to photocopy) © Thomas R. Black 1993

Article/Report: _____

Question/hypothesis (Actions 1–3/Ch. 2)	Representativeness (Actions 4–5/Ch. 3)	Data Quality I (Action 6/Ch. 4)	Data Quality II (Action 6/Ch. 4)	Descriptive Statistics (Action 7/Ch. 5)	Inferential Statistical Analysis (Action 7/Chs 6 & 7)
Valid question or hypothesis based on accepted theory with well-justified referenced support	Whole population	Educationally, sociologically, psychologically etc. significant and manageable number of concepts	Commercially produced and tested with high validity, reliability and objectivity (V, R, O)	Appropriate display of data and results	Appropriate choice of design, and sound H_0
Valid question or hypothesis based on own theory, well justified	Random selection from a specified population	Limited academic significance, very narrow perspective	Project produced and tested with high V, R, O	Some inadequacies, incorrectness in data/results display	A more powerful test could have been used
Credible question/ hypothesis but alternatives possible, or too extensive/global, or support missing	Purposive sampling from a specified population	Large number of concepts, potentially confusing	Commercially or project produced with moderate V, R, O	Other methods of display data/results would be more appropriate	Missing analysis where needed
Weak question/ hypothesis, or poorly stated, or justified with inappropriate references	Volunteers	Too many concepts and variables investigated to result in any meaning	Commercially or project produced with low V, R, O or no information provided	Serious misconceptions through use of descriptive statistics	Inappropriately analysed, tests performed not appropriate
No question or hypothesis stated, or inconsistent with known facts	Unidentified group	Trivial concepts, not academically significant	Inappropriate instrument for this application	Intentionally misleading use of descriptive statistics	No justification for analysis, post hoc data snooping

Comments:

8
Controlling Variables and Drawing Conclusions

Up to this point, a wide variety of interrelated criteria for judging the appropriateness of the design and employment of sampling techniques, measuring instruments, presentation of data and statistical tests has been introduced. Interrelationships have been identified as often as possible, showing where decisions at one level will affect the quality of the procedure at another, which in turn will affect the *strength* of the inferences and conclusions the researcher can make. The main problem is that usually it is just its relative value that is affected and rarely is a piece of research totally useless. This places the onus on the reader to decide just how much value to place on a given piece of research when citing it as a basis or justification of his or her own study. This is not a trivial decision and one that requires careful consideration. Just how far from the ideal can the procedure of a study deviate and still be used as a valid reference? By now, the criteria in the previous seven chapters should have been applied to a variety of articles. This alone should provide you with some insight into the answer to this question, since every situation is going to be different.

It must be remembered that research is a continuing process, social science research rarely produces earth-shaking discoveries, and every researcher builds on the work of others, no matter how imperfect it may be. As researchers, we should all be able to learn from our own and others' mistakes. Ideally, it is the researcher's task to collect (in a replicable manner) and present evidence dispassionately. It is recognized that it is impossible to separate researchers from their beliefs, particularly since these are often the motivation for carrying out the research. Yet most researchers should endeavour to carry out their research in such a way as to survive public scrutiny and not produce unwarranted conclusions. As a reader, you will have to contend with the imperfect real world, with a knowledge gained from this text of what ought to be. To this end, this final chapter will bring together the criteria presented so far, showing how earlier procedures in a research project can affect the appropriateness and strength of conclusions in reports.

Cause and effect

There are a number of ways to maintain 'control' over variables, ensuring that the effect observed is due to the limited number in which the researcher is interested and not some others. Primarily this is achieved through sampling in *ex post facto* studies employing quasi-experimental designs, whereas true experimental studies will require some form of random distribution of subjects across groups to receive some treatment. All studies endeavour to avoid the effects of unwanted variables by careful design and administration of the measuring instruments. Yet structuring a study so that it is possible to justify any tendency for cause and effect relationships requires the researcher to plan and execute the study with extreme care.

Statements often appear in reports such as 'there was a significant difference between the scores of two groups', which subsequently is used to justify the existence of a cause and effect relationship between the two variables. Unfortunately, many of the events in the world, particularly those influenced by people, have multiple causes and many that may not be at all obvious. This is partly due to the fact that the events do not occur with the definite predictability of everyday happenings. For example, when someone hits a table with a hammer, unless you are deaf, you will hear a noise. The probabilistic world is equivalent to expecting a noise, but recognizing that there is a finite probability there will not be one. In statistically based social science research, the problem is even more complicated: while statistical significance does tell us that whatever difference that exists probably did not occur by chance alone, it does not tell us what did cause the difference. This is somewhat like watching a magician for whom one has a considerable amount of suspicion: if he hits the watch rolled up in the cloth with a hammer, is the noise we hear that of the hammer hitting the watch? The proof may require careful investigation to confirm or refute what the appropriate inference is (what caused the sound) for our observation (seeing the cloth struck and hearing the sound). While the magician may deny us the opportunity for closer observation, the researcher when writing a report should not.

Let us consider a simple example. If you measure how tall all the 12-year-olds and 8-year-olds in a school are, within each group the heights will not be the same. While 12-year-olds will *tend* to be taller than the 8-year-olds, not all the children in the older group will be taller than all those in the younger group. Age is not related to a certain single height. Even if a representative group of all children having the same birth date were chosen, the heights would vary. Not surprisingly, if a graph were plotted of the heights versus number of people for a large sample, we would find that the heights would vary normally around a mean for an age group. Also, the mean height of the 12-year-olds would probably exceed that of the 8-year-olds, and a statistical test (for example, a *t*-test) would show that they did indeed not belong to the same population for height. But from these data alone, we are still none the wiser as to the *cause* of the differences in height, either within the groups or between the groups.

While direct cause and effect is difficult to define in the same way as the sound produced by a hammer, we can say that there is a *tendency* for older children to be taller than younger children, based on observations such as those described. Still, age itself does not cause a child to be taller, there are underlying biological processes that are the actual cause; age is only a convenient marker. What makes it even more difficult to analyse is the fact that we all have known an 8-year-old who was taller than a 12-year-old.

Carrying the example one step further, let us now introduce an imaginary situation; in visits to classes of 12-year-olds, a researcher unexpectedly visits a class that has a mean height of one metre (think about it: these kids are short!). By taking the mean and standard deviation of such a group and comparing it to population parameters using a z-test, it is possible to determine the probability of this group of 30 short students belonging to the overall population of 12-year-olds, at least with respect to this single trait. In reality, they could be a concentrated group out in the tail of that distribution. If the probability that they are part of the main population is less than 5 per cent (one in 20), then it is significant, which is likely in this case. In other words, we would reject the null hypothesis that the group is not different from the whole population. Well, the researcher, wanting to be *really* sure, sets the significance level at 1 per cent. In other words, if the probability that this group of apparently exceptionally short students is part of the population of 12-year-olds is less than 1 per cent, he will reject the null hypothesis (that they are not different) and accept there is a difference. Theoretically, there is no such thing as a zero probability, the tails of the bell-shaped curve never reach zero, never touching the horizontal line, they just get closer and closer. But we know that in reality, there is a tallest and a shortest (see, for example, the *Guinness Book of Records.*)

Assuming that the researcher has found a statistically significantly different group of exceptionally short 12-year-olds, the question arises, what does it mean? It is probably easier to tell what it does not mean. The statistical significance does not tell us the cause of this shortness, and any researcher trying to ascertain the cause will have to be a good detective to isolate it. And there is the real chance that there is no individual cause. Also, there is the finite probability (one in a 100) that this collection of short 12-year-olds in one place is perfectly 'normal', and it is only a chance occurrence (remote as it may be) that these short 12-year-olds are all in the same class in a school. The statistical test strongly suggests that this is highly unlikely, but it is possible. Now as the researcher is only an observer of life and must employ an *ex post facto* design, it is much more difficult to prove that any cause(s) he might identify are the correct ones and not something else, since he has no control over competing variables.

Following the case of the short 12-year-olds a bit further, the researcher proceeds to search for a cause. Through questionnaires and interviews, he discovers that all their parents work at the local bean canning factory and, therefore, have as a bonus a free supply of beans. Since salaries are low, understandably the families eat considerable quantities of beans, again (statistically) significantly more than the national average. Is this the cause of the observed short stature? Our researcher is now obliged to investigate a multitude of other possible causes, ranging from genetics to diet to water, and is unlikely to isolate a single cause in such an *ex post facto* study. Even if a diet of beans were the physiological 'cause', this might satisfy the biologist, but not others. Would a sociologist accept this or prefer to attribute the cause to the position of the parents in the class structure of society? Would an educationist prefer to attribute the cause to lack of knowledge and understanding of proper diet? Would a psychologist wish to pursue the approach that it was manipulation by the bean factory and the parents were inappropriately convinced of the value of a high bean diet, or enticed to eat beans? Each discipline brings along its own perspective of the world, which can influence conclusions.

This conveniently leads to the reason there is such an interest in true experimental designs. If an experiment is performed where the researcher has control over the independent variables (the possible causes), then justifiably drawing conclusions is a little easier. For our example, it would be advantageous to be able to take a random sample of newborn children from all over the country and raise them on varying proportions of beans in their diet, and monitor their growth over time, but ethics prevent this. Would guinea pigs do for an experiment? Or monkeys? It is apparent that the problem is not with the statistics, it is with the multitude of possible variables and the difficulty in actually carrying out what appears to be the most satisfactory experiment. Studies in the social sciences are no easier to devise. In such situations, it may be that detective techniques based on better-designed *ex post facto* studies and other investigative procedures will be needed to resolve the dilemma as to the cause of the observed effect.

The challenge for readers of research reports is to decide how well the researcher has accounted for all the possible causes and how well he or she has justified the identification of the cause of the observed effect, if this is the case. When a report omits a discussion on this, then the reader begins to wonder about the quality of the research and/or the depth of understanding about research design possessed by the researcher. Later discussion will point up some subtle and not so subtle potential sources of weak and inadequate conclusions. In addition, readers would reasonably expect a conscientious researcher to identify limitations of the present study and make recommendations for further work.

Controlling variables

To be able to justify adequately any cause and effect relations, a researcher aims to 'control' all the variables in a study. This requires that he or she ensures that the desired independent variables do have the opportunity to demonstrate an effect on the measured outcome (dependent variable) and eliminates any possible influence by any other specific potential independent variables. There are two basic ways to accomplish this: (a) as seen in

Chapter 7, design the study actually to use certain characteristics of the sample group as possible independent variables to see if these affect the measured dependent variables; and (b) randomly select or distribute the sample(s) essentially to spread all other possible variables evenly across all groups. Thus, the more complex the study, like multidimensional factorial analysis of variance, the more variables one is trying to control by observing their possible influence on the measured dependent variable. The simpler the study, such as a *t*-test comparing two groups, the more variables one is trying to account for through random sampling.

Thus, if a study is centred on one set of potential independent variables, those others recognized by the theory being applied as affecting the dependent variables being studied are considered to be *mediating variables*. For example, a study investigating the effect of a new learning situation would want to ensure that each group was initially the same with respect to distribution of intelligence (thus one group should not have a higher mean IQ test score), previous learning, interest in the subject matter, resources available outside the learning situation etc.

To illustrate this further, consider the researcher who wishes to investigate possible variables influencing the cognitive emphasis of examinations given by university teachers. In other words, having seen professors' and lecturers' examinations, why do some papers demand much more intellectually of the learners, and consequently have a larger proportion of questions requiring problem-solving than others? There are a number of possible independent variables: age, sex, academic background, subject taught, size of institution, years of non-academic and academic experience etc. Even choosing the three potential independent variables: academic experience (0–2 years, 3–10 years, 10 or more years), subject taught (science, engineering, humanities) and size of institution (less than 5,000 students, 5,000–10,000 students, over 10,000 students) means a $3 \times 3 \times 3$ design, as shown in Figure 8.1. This would allow one to check not only the possible influence of each of these variables individually, but also combinations of variables (the interactions represented by the 27 individual cells in the matrix), on the proportion of problem-solving questions included on examination papers. Thus, not only could one test whether or not different levels of experience had any effect on question asking, but also whether one combination of experience, size of institution and subject had more of an effect than another combination. Unfortunately, there would be 351 possible pair-wise comparisons! The problem then becomes one of making sense of the results. For example, taking just one of these possible pair-wise combinations, what would one say about the result showing that science teachers with 3–10 years' experience at institutions of 5,000–10,000 students ask significantly more problem-solving questions than humanities teachers with 0–2 years' experience at institutions with 0–5,000 students? This forces us to return to the original plan: were the hypotheses and variables well thought out in the first place?

Returning to the design, it still would be necessary to control the

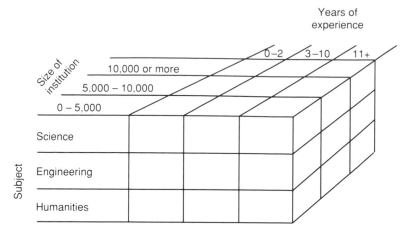

Figure 8.1   *A 3 × 3 × 3 design with percentage of problem-solving questions on examinations as the dependent variable.*

possible influence of the other potential independent mediating variables mentioned by random sampling. This would mean each cell would have lecturers of both sexes, of a range of ages, having a variety of academic qualifications etc., in other words typical of lecturers and professors in general. To have a sound sample, it would be preferable to have 30 subjects in each of the 27 cells, or 810 persons! Even if these were randomly selected from institutions, it is likely not all will respond to the request for sample examinations, so that the percentage of questions at higher levels can be determined (dependent variable).

Taking this example on one more stage: when applying for a grant to carry out this investigation, the researcher gets significantly less funding than the sum requested (not surprising). The consequence is that there are resources for a study of 100 lecturers, so it is decided to investigate only one variable, academic subject (three cells). Thus the role of sampling requires that all the other mediating variables (including type of institution and years of experience) be accounted for by the representativeness. Consequently, in each cell, there will now also be lecturers from all three sizes of institution having years of experience 'typical' of academics. Though this design does not allow the researcher to comment on any potential contribution of the variables, size of institution and relative amount of experience, these have been controlled. Alternatively, the researcher could have fewer academics in each cell for a two-dimensional design (9 cells with 11 each), but finding significance will be more difficult in that the differences in mean number of questions will have to be greater than for larger cell sizes.

In addition, there are other variables that can affect the outcome(s) of any study. The actual mechanism of collecting the data can interfere with the quality of the results and affect the validity, reliability and objectivity of the data and, consequently, the validity of any conclusions. For example, the time at which a test is given, questionnaire completed, or observations are made could inadvertently introduce a variable that could affect the results. Such a variable might be introduced in such an obvious way as measuring some of the subjects before lunch and some after, or a much more subtle influence such as the presence of an observer, which can affect the performance of some tasks. Such variables not included in the theory or model underlying the study that could influence the outcomes are known as *extraneous variables*.

Most of these have been mentioned in conjunction with aspects of research design described in earlier chapters, but Campbell and Stanley (1963) have provided a succinct list of 12 factors that can jeopardize validity. These were expanded to 13 by Cohen and Manion (1989), which are divided below into two categories: internal and external validity. When possible interactions are added, there are 15 potential sources of confounding.

Internal validity refers to the design of the study and collection of the data. These can be adversely influenced by eight extraneous variables, which will be potentially present to varying degrees, depending upon the design of the study. The first four pertain specifically to designs that include subjects being 'measured' more than once (test then re-test). The others are relevant to almost any design.

1 *History*. Something other than what was intended happens to the subjects between the first test or observation and the second that produces an effect(s) that can be confused with that produced by the independent variable(s). This could range from members of a group watching a television programme to political events.

2 *Maturation*. As the name indicates, the subjects mature in some way, becoming older, wiser, hungrier or even more tired. As can be seen, the time scale will depend upon the nature of the variables involved and could be as short as minutes or as long as years.

3 *Testing*. Sometimes the actual measuring instrument will affect the outcome(s) on a second, later measure. For example, this could involve subjects actually learning some subject matter from a test, the instrument could constitute practice of a skill in itself, or subjects might infer the purpose of a questionnaire and subsequently answer in the manner they think the experimenter wants (or does not want). Recall the example of the considerable discrepancy between pollsters' predictions and the actual outcome in the parliamentary election of 1992 in Britain described in Chapter 4.

4 *Statistical regression*. There is a tendency for some traits to have subjects regress towards the mean with increasing time. In other words, those who did well on the first achievement test tend to come closer to the mean the second time; those that score low on an attitude survey the first time will score close to the mean the second.

5 *Instrumentation.* The measuring instruments lack reliability, either inherently or over time. Observers may change their criteria or simply flag with time. This can be checked through the various means of determining the reliability coefficient for an instrument discussed in Chapter 4.

6 *Selection bias.* This is particularly apparent when established groups are selected to be experimental or control groups, subsequently subjected to some experience, then measured: whether it was the experience or the original group characteristics that made the difference becomes unclear. This is one of the reasons for random assignment to groups (Chapter 3).

7 *Experimental mortality.* Even if one starts with random selection or assignment to groups, there will sometimes be attrition, loss of subjects. Those that are left may well be a different group from that originally selected and mediating variables may no longer be accounted for. Knowing why subjects dropped out can help to discount this extraneous variable, particularly if it can be shown that the reason had nothing to do with the study. Large numbers of subjects can also minimize any effects. This was mentioned earlier with respect to designs comparing two independent groups (Chapter 6).

8 *Interactions of 1–7.* For example, selection bias may interact with maturation in such a way as to produce confounding effects.

In addition, there are seven factors (adapted from Campbell and Stanley, 1963, and Cohen and Manion, 1989) that would affect *external validity*, or generalizability of the results:

9 *Reactive or interaction effect of testing.* This is particularly relevant to experimental designs where the first measurement increases or decreases the subjects' sensitivity to whatever the experimental treatment is. For example, a before-experience attitude questionnaire could make subjects more sensitive to the experience than in non-experimental situations. Thus, the experiment would not be comparable to real life and the results could not be generalized to the population from which the sample was taken.

10 *Multiple-treatment interference.* Some studies involve multiple treatments over time and the effects of earlier treatments are not erasable. This is particularly true for single groups in learning situations: determining which treatment after the first is the determining factor will be difficult.

11 *Inadequate operational definition of dependent variable.* This can result in the effect only being seen in experimental situations and not in real life. For example, career choice indicated on a questionnaire may not be matched by true commitment or ability to pursue that career in reality. This is one of the reasons for the emphasis on validity of operational definitions in Chapter 4.

12 *Inadequate definition of independent variable.* If the categories to which subjects are assigned are not clearly defined, it will not be possible to replicate the study. For example, there is considerable disagreement about how social classes are defined among sociologists, thus one would expect an explicit operation definition in any study employing this concept.

13 *Lack of representativeness of sample.* The sample may not be representative of any population, as discussed in Chapter 3. All too often it could be described as 'convenience sampling', using a convenient group, which means that the researcher is really using a whole population, should not be using inferential statistical tests and will not be able to generalize legitimately to any larger group.

14 *The Hawthorn effect.* Just knowing that they are part of an experiment can sometimes affect the performance of subjects and contaminate results. Double-blind designs that result in no one knowing who is in the experimental group and who is in the control group are widely used in medicine to control for psychological affects interfering with medicinal ones. This is more difficult to achieve in social science designs.

15 *Interaction of extraneous variables (9–14 above) and experimental variables.* Sample selection bias, for example, could influence the effect of an experimental treatment, making it impossible to tell which was the cause of the observed result.

Obviously, there are numerous potential sources of confounding of results, so that even if one does find a statistically significant result, it will take considerable care to ensure that the identified independent variable is the real cause. The reader will not always be able to determine the validity of claims from the information provided in the report or article, but the above does provide an indication of key points to look for when considering a document.

Put in more mathematical terms, Kerlinger (1986) makes the point that the choice of research design and subsequent statistical test is based upon having as great a control over variance as possible: 'Maximise systematic variance, control extraneous variance, and minimise error variance.' These all relate to issues raised earlier;

(a) To maximize systematic variance indicates a need to make sure that as much of the variability round the mean as possible is attributable to those variables in which the researcher is interested.

(b) To control extraneous variance can be interpreted to indicate a need to reduce the amount of variability of scores round the mean that can be attributed to extraneous variables as much as possible.

(c) To minimize error variance requires that the measuring instruments are as reliable as possible (recall how reliability coefficients are calculated).

These are of primary importance to parametric statistical tests since they employ variance (standard deviation squared) in the calculations and decisions about significance levels.

Criteria for evaluating variable control

In summary of the above, the following are the criteria for this column of the Profiling Sheet.

All mediating and extraneous variables accounted for, internal validity maintained. A reader would expect to find a detailed description of the design of the study that described the theory including all possible variables, noted those to be included in the study and how mediating variables were to be controlled, provided sufficient information to have a high mark in the Data Quality II column, and indicated how extraneous variables were controlled.

Most mediating and extraneous variables accounted for. The degree of transgression or omission that will be tolerated is up to the reader. Obviously, most studies will not be perfect, but you will have to decide whether this or the next is appropriate. Comments entered on the Profiling Sheet would clarify such a classification.

Mediating variables controlled only, confounding possible. The researcher has not controlled extraneous variables, thus leaving the source of the effect unclear. Comments as to what you think are the confounding variables would be appropriate.

Inadequate control of variables, confounding probable. Not only are extraneous variables not accounted for, but mediating variables have not been controlled. Sometimes this results from lack of a clear model or theory, or a lack of a clear research question and hypothesis.

Control of mediating and extraneous variables not discussed, confounding possible. Sometimes this results from a lack of understanding of research processes, or there is a deficiency in writing skills to convey what has been done. Whatever the cause, it is not clear that any variables have been controlled, though something has happened to the subjects and data have been collected; just what has been done to avoid confounding is not clear.

Drawing conclusions

There is a statement supposedly made by a politician that there was a definite problem with the Navy since half the sailors were below the Navy's average for intelligence! (If you did not laugh, recall what the mean tells us; see Chapter 5.) This points up two main sources of problems that researchers will encounter when drawing conclusions from a measurement-based study: (a) a basic understanding of (or lack of) what research and statistics can tell us; and (b) the problems of controlling extraneous and mediating variables. These ultimately end up being linked when one finds a study making unwarranted claims.

One suspected source of unreasonable conclusions (here is a study in itself!) is the ubiquitous computer and the vast amount of statistical software available to help carry out calculations. As has been noted already, it is all too easy for a researcher (if he or she can be called that) to collect data unsystematically, trot over to the computer centre, and find a friendly soul who will help enter the data into an apparently appropriate program that will do all the number crunching. Out comes the statistical significance, but what does it all mean? The reason for this speculation comes from reading articles that in one sentence state 'and the difference was significant at the 5 per cent level ($p < 0.05$)', followed by the claim 'thus we can safely say that A caused B'. There is no mention of mediating or extraneous variables, and sometimes the sample description leaves much to be desired. Statistical tests only confirm that whatever was observed did or did not (probably) happen by chance alone, indicating indirectly how likely that there was a cause. Justification of the cause is a matter for the researcher. It also seems a shame to read a report that appears to be the product of a conscientious researcher who has carefully designed instruments and collected data, only to have left it unprotected at the computer centre, allowing someone else to 'squeeze as much as possible out of the data'. A researcher does not have to be a computer wizard to use this tool properly, just informed about what a statistical test will reveal, and to be able to defend his or her choice.

The last column of the Profiling Sheet could be considered as the summary of all the others. Having arrived at the end of the report or article you are asking, what relative value will I place on these findings? How much will they influence my own research and thinking? There are few perfect reports and there are few totally useless ones, at least in refereed journals, thus the evaluation should rarely result in a binary classification of rubbish or perfect. Evaluation implies careful analysis, identification of implied meanings, and deciding how well supported the results and conclusions are. To make matters more complex, the justification for any conclusions is not given just at the end of a report or article; the entire structure of the study and procedure followed constitute part of the justification (or limitations) of the results. The processes involved are much too complex, as this book has endeavoured to demonstrate, to allow the rationalization of results to be confined to a few sentences.

Some common pitfalls

While the following list is not exhaustive, it does include many of the common sources of misleading conclusions in reports and articles (Blum and Foos, 1986; Cohen and Manion 1989; Shipman, 1972).

1   Inadequate theoretical framework leads to poorly or weakly defined variables, for example, teacher effectiveness, social class, intelligence (IQ tests are not the only measure), violence on television (are Bugs Bunny and Rambo equally violent?), levels of crime or unemployment, to mention a few.

2   The conclusion refers only to data that support the hypothesis. There is a difficulty in detecting this in a journal article, but it may be more apparent when referring to the full report, thesis or dissertation behind it. Too often, beliefs govern what is selectively reported.

3   Conclusions are extended to individual behaviour when the study has focused on group tendencies. Statistical studies involve data collected on groups and the tests of significance use means and standard deviations, for example, thus individuals within the groups will perform/behave divergently, providing variance round a mean. To use a mean as an indicator of expected individual behaviour/performance is inappropriate. For example, if the average annual income of accountants were £25,000, would you expect your neighbour Fred the accountant to make exactly £25,000?

4   The conclusion appears to ignore the data and yet includes arguments for the support of the original hypothesis in the face of negative evidence. The first possible reason for this is a lack of logical consistency in the report. Blum and Foos (1986) describe this as a form of rationalism, which can degenerate into a set of excuses for not finding what was expected. On the other hand, it is possible that the researcher is being honest about procedural faults, documents them, and is actually suggesting a replication of the study to resolve this issue. Considering the complexity of social science research, it is surprising that more of this type of evaluation of procedure does not occur.

5   Even with a non-representative sample, conclusions are extended to a larger population (see Chapter 2). This happens all too often when a convenient group or volunteers are used as subjects for a study. Even when a research project starts with a random selection of subjects, often there is some attrition. As long as there is a follow-up of those who did not continue, and the reason they did not participate had nothing to do with what was happening to them as part of the study, then there is still justification for extending the results to the original population. For example, questionnaires can be lost in the post, subjects become ill or move, jobs or roles change which can make their participation inappropriate or impossible. If the reason for not continuing is not identified, then there is always the suspicion that something going on in the study has caused them to drop out, like the wording of a questionnaire, reluctance to be observed in the manner planned, or their role in an experiment. In such cases, the research approach itself could have provided a confounding variable.

6   The conclusions are based upon the researchers applying their own operational definition to a set of existing statistics. In other words, the data were collected by another group, for example government statistical offices

collecting census data, and the researchers assign their own meaning, such as using income as the sole indicator of social class. The study then reports various correlations with other data (again defined by the researchers as indicators of their own variables) and conclusions are reported. While this may seem harmless, the reader must be assured that such definitions are valid. Wide-searching surveys are often conducted as a general data trawl, though sometimes there are hypotheses to be tested. Government agencies are looking for trends in society to predict housing, school and medical needs for coming years. Reports using such data for some other purpose should stimulate the reader to ask searching questions about the validity of the operational definitions.

7   Conclusions sometimes include an attempt to relate the study's findings to other studies. Unless there has been a definite effort to replicate a study, the reader ought to ensure that the data (operational definitions) are comparable. There are frequent problems when trying to make cross-cultural or cross-national comparisons, for example when difficult to define variables such as social class are employed. Does 'lower middle class' mean the same thing in Spain as in Canada, for example? Such problems can occur with longitudinal studies where definitions can change over time. Are teachers, civil servants or doctors as 'well off' today as they were 100 years ago? Has the purchasing power of the middle class improved or declined since the Second World War? How purchasing power is defined by those who collect the two sets of data will determine the relative validity of any conclusions.

8   There are still occasional papers in which the conclusions confuse statistical significance with sociological, psychological or educational significance. If a study were to show that the reading age of 12-year-old girls was 2 per cent higher than that for 12-year-old boys (assume that the difference was statistically different), is this educationally significant? Should a national programme be started to rescue boys from a fate worse than death? This is not to say there is not a difference, but is it large enough to generate any concern?

9   Conclusions have been known to provide claims that go beyond the evidence provided, taking one more 'logical' step. For example, if a study were to show that there was a high positive correlation between the number of books in homes and the ultimate achievement of educational qualifications, is it reasonable to recommend that sets of books should be given to families that lack sufficient reading material?

10   It is still possible to find conclusions that automatically attribute cause and effect relations for simple correlations, just because the correlations are significant. As seen in Chapter 6, correlations are an indication of strength of association, but by no means proof of cause and effect.

11   Parallel to the previous item, there are conclusions that maintain a cause and effect relationship for experimental or quasi-experimental studies based on finding statistical significance alone. Again, as noted in

Chapters 6 and 7 and earlier in this chapter, the burden of proof rests with the researcher, who must prove that all other possible causes have been controlled, *and* even then should really only state the relationship in probabilistic terms.

With time and experience, you surely will be able to add to this list.

Criteria for evaluating conclusions

The following are summary criteria for the last column on the Profiling Sheet:

Appropriately drawn based on data shown. A well-designed and executed study, not necessarily using inferential statistics, but clear in its presentation, defending and justifying any conclusions, basically a sound study worth referring to in your own research.

Some lack justification or are poorly defended. Not all the conclusions are fully justified or some are poorly defended. This could be due to a weak design (see other columns) or poor writing ability of the researcher.

No justification of conclusions. The results and conclusions are presented, but no justification is given for these. This requires the reader to 'read between the lines' to try to infer why, and to consider the design, sampling and data collection procedures carefully to determine whether the conclusions are justified. This can be due to something being hidden, but, more than likely, it is poor writing ability.

No conclusions drawn, only description of data and process. Some reports of studies (but very few articles) lack any real conclusions. These tend to present the data but draw no substantive conclusions nor make any recommendations. This can indicate a poor design, lack of initial research question or hypothesis, and/or poor data collection procedures.

Inappropriate conclusions for data. Occasionally, a research paper draws conclusions that are not substantiated by the results presented. The researcher goes well beyond what is justifiable from the study at hand.

Summary

How you, the reader, intend to use the result may well influence how you ultimately rate overall a given report or journal article. If you are carrying out a literature search, looking for justification for your own research, then you may tend to be more lenient in your classification, or at least in how much credence you attribute to a weak study. On the other hand, if you are an administrator or teacher looking for justification of a change, for example in policy, administrative structure or teaching style, then the strength of the supporting evidence for conclusions must be very strong.

Belief may be a great motivator, but evidence to the contrary should not be ignored.

The aim of this book has been to provide comprehensive coverage and, consequently, some readers will require a greater depth of understanding for particular topics to be found in more advanced texts. Quantitative studies in the social sciences are complex, partly because using numbers requires some understanding of the mathematics behind their use, and partly because such studies contend with very difficult subjects: human beings. It is hoped that this book will help you the reader overcome any reluctance to read quantitative studies and, for some of you, help you on the road to competently designing and carrying out your own studies. You should now be well equipped to tackle Activity 8.1.

Activity 8.1

Select a completely new article/report and carry out a full evaluation using the entire Profiling Sheet at the end of this chapter.

Finally, by keeping your expectations of quality of research high and communicating this to such bodies as the editorial boards of journals, you will be contributing to the improvement of quantitative research: which is an interesting hypothesis for someone's research!

References

Blum, M.L. and Foos, P.W. (1986) *Gathering Data: Experimental Methods Plus*. Harper & Row.

Campbell, D.T. and Stanley, J.C. (1963) *Experimental and Quasi-experimental Designs for Research*. Rand McNally.

Cohen, L. and Manion, L. (1989) *Research Methods in Education*, 3rd edn. Routledge.

Kerlinger, F.N. (1986) *Foundations of Behavioral Research*, 3rd edn. Holt, Rinehart & Winston.

Shipman, M.D. (1972) *The Limitations of Social Research*. Longman.

Profiling Sheet: Evaluating Social Science Research (to photocopy) © Thomas R. Black 1993

Article/Report: _____

Question/hypothesis (Actions 1–3/Ch. 2)	Representativeness (Actions 4–5/Ch. 3)	Data Quality I (Action 6/Ch. 4)	Data Quality II (Action 6/Ch. 4)	Descriptive Statistics (Action 7/Ch. 5)	Inferential Statistical Analysis (Action 7/Chs. 6 & 7)	Variable Control (Action 8/Ch. 8)	Data Analysis and Conclusions (Action 8/Ch. 8)
Valid question or hypothesis based on accepted theory with well-justified referenced support	Whole population	Educationally, sociologically, psychologically etc. significant and manageable number of concepts	Commercially produced and tested with high validity, reliability and objectivity (V, R, O)	Appropriate display of data and results	Appropriate choice of design, and sound H_0	All mediating and extraneous variables accounted for, internal validity maintained	Appropriately drawn based on data shown
Valid question or hypothesis based on own theory, well justified	Random selection from a specified population	Limited academic significance, very narrow perspective	Project produced and tested with high V, R, O	Some inadequacies, incorrectness in data/results display	A more powerful test could have been used	Most mediating and extraneous variables accounted for	Some lack justification or are poorly defended
Credible question/ hypothesis but alternatives possible, or too extensive/global, or support missing	Purposive sampling from a specified population	Large number of concepts, potentially confusing	Commercially or project produced with moderate V, R, O	Other methods of display data/results would be more appropriate	Missing analysis where needed	Mediating variables controlled only, confounding possible	No justification of conclusions
Weak question/ hypothesis, or poorly stated, or justified with inappropriate references	Volunteers	Too many concepts and variables investigated to result in any meaning	Commercially or project produced with low V, R, O or no information provided	Serious misconceptions through use of descriptive statistics	Inappropriately analysed, tests performed not appropriate	Inadequate control of variables, confounding probable	No conclusions drawn, only description of data and process
No question or hypothesis stated, or inconsistent with known facts	Unidentified group	Trivial concepts, not academically significant	Inappropriate instrument for this application	Intentionally misleading use of descriptive statistics	No justification for analysis, *post hoc* data snooping	Control of mediating and extraneous variables not discussed, confounding possible	Inappropriate conclusions for data

Comments:

Index